I must be
talking to myself

*Dialogue in the Roman Catholic Church
since Vatican II*

MARK PATRICK HEDERMAN

VERITAS

First published 2004 by
Veritas Publications
7/8 Lower Abbey Street
Dublin 1
Ireland
Email publications@veritas.ie
Website www.veritas.ie

ISBN 1 85390 747 2

Cover design by Bill Bolger
Printed in the Republic of Ireland by the Leinster Leader, Dublin

*Veritas books are printed on paper made from the wood pulp of managed
forests. For every tree felled, at least one tree is planted, thereby renewing
natural resources.*

CONTENTS

PREFACE

It is forty years since the Second Vatican Council promulgated its Decree on Ecumenism on November 21, 1964. The opening words of papal encyclicals are normally used as titles and so the opening words of this conciliar document, *Unitatis Redintegratio*, or Restoration of Unity, have become familiar. However, its official title is the Decree on Ecumenism. Whatever about the title, the issue here is about the reality. Does ecumenism still exist? What has happened to Roman Catholic dialogue with other Christians, with non-Christians (if religions other than Christianity will allow such a patronising and generic term), with atheists? It was this official document that made such dialogue possible for Roman Catholics for the first time forty years ago. 'This is more than the opening of a door; new ground has been broken,' said Dr Oscar Cullmann, a Protestant observer at the Council. 'No Catholic document,' he went on to say, 'has ever spoken of non-Catholic Christians in this way.' Was it a mistake, a hiatus, a ploy? 'The test of the Decree will be found in what now happens in local communities', Samuel McCrea Cavert wrote in his response to the document published in English by Austin Flannery in 1966. The purpose of this book is to re-examine the document itself, situate it in its historical context, describe what happened to it in official Roman Catholic teaching since its appearance, and find out whether it is still alive and well in 2004. The word around which such probing must pivot is 'dialogue'. This was the buzz word in the 1960s. What did it mean then? What does it mean now? Did it ever add anything new to Roman Catholic teaching or theology? Or was it simply a fashionable slogan harnessed to a more salubriously oiled propaganda machine?

I wrote the bulk of this present book twenty years ago. At the time I was secretary to the Glenstal Ecumenical Conference. This conference opened in the year the Decree on Ecumenism was promulgated. The Glenstal Ecumenical Conference provided the occasion for Church of Ireland, Presbyterian and Methodist Christians to meet together with some Roman Catholics for the first time in Ireland on 26 June 1964. The conference has been held every year since then. This year, 2004, therefore, we also celebrate its fortieth anniversary. Before our twentieth anniversary in 1983 I was invited to form an *ad hoc* interdenominational committee to offer suggestions as to the future. My report was published in October 1983.[1] It seemed to the committee that some radical steps would have to be taken. 'What we propose is that this conference set itself as its immediate task and its long-term goal the study and resolution of the problem of inter-communion between the different denominations which attend. We also propose that the twenty-first Glenstal Ecumenical Conference should not be held until it is possible for us to celebrate a Eucharist in which all members might participate fully. Such an event would really mark our coming of age and our opinion is that we should postpone this twenty-first birthday for whatever time is necessary – even if it be five or ten years – until such a common celebration of our maturity is possible.' A panel of experts was established to formulate an agreed text for a common Eucharist. The Rev. Dr John M. Barkley (Presbyterian); Dean Gilbert Mayes (Church of Ireland); The Rev. Robert Nelson (Methodist); and Dom Placid Murray, OSB, of Glenstal Abbey

(Roman Catholic) drew up and presented to the Standing Committee of the Ecumenical Conference a Proposed Text for a Common Eucharist in May 1985. The text was adopted by the Committee and was used for a common celebration of the Eucharist with permission from the then Roman Catholic Archbishop of Cashel and Emly, Thomas Morris, and the authorities from the other four participating denominations. The Abbot of Glenstal, now Abbot President of the Congregation of the Annunciation, Dom Celestine Cullen was Chief Celebrant, with concelebrating ministers from Church of Ireland, Presbyterian and Methodist clergy, while all members of the Conference, apart from two conscientious objectors, one Roman Catholic, one Presbyterian, received communion.

This was certainly a high point of ecumenism in my own lifetime and, in my understanding, a miraculous work of the Holy Spirit. Dialogue throughout these forty years of the Glenstal Conference has made me aware, in a way that no theology, text or academic argument could do, that the Holy Spirit is alive and present in Christian Churches other than the Roman Catholic. By the Spirit's fruits you shall know the Holy Spirit. These are the persons you meet who have allowed their persons to become one with the Person of the Holy Spirit. So many of the people attending this ecumenical conference so faithfully over the last forty years have been proof of this presence of the Holy Spirit. And I will certainly go to my grave in deepest gratitude to that same Holy Spirit for the gift that it was to share communion once on earth as prelude to the communion that I shall undoubtedly share with these same Christian persons for the whole of eternity.

Since then the same eucharistic sharing has not been possible. This is for myriad reasons: theological, political, psychological, practical. Essentially we do not recognise one another's ministry. The Roman Catholic Church recognises the baptism of other Christians, but not their ordination to the one Priesthood of Christ.

So, once again, now forty rather than twenty years later, we pose the question '*Quo vadimus?*'

This book, which was offered for publication twenty years ago and turned down, has been resurrected by the publisher and I have been asked to rewrite it and bring it up to date. So, here it is. May it help to bring us all to fullest communion with each other.

Notes

1   Mark Patrick Hederman, 'The Future of Glenstal Ecumenical Congress', *Doctrine and Life*, October, 1983, pp. 486-490.

CHAPTER I

GENESIS OF 'DIALOGUE'

It is not possible to trace the genesis of the term 'dialogue' as it was used in the council documents of Vatican II. The document on ecumenism, unlike the document on the liturgy, was not the result of long and laborious effort on the part of recognized and established groups working within the Church. Apart from a handful of courageous and isolated pioneers such as Cardinal Mercier, L'Abbé Portal, L'Abbé Coutourier and Dom Lambert Baudouin, the whole notion of ecumenism was a comparative novelty in Catholic theology before Vatican II.

Many would claim that the notion of 'dialogue', as it was incorporated into *Lumen Gentium, Gaudium et Spes* and the Decree on Ecumenism itself, was the result of a direct if somewhat vague inspiration of Pope John XXIII. Be that as it may, it is clear from even a cursory reading of the pronouncements and the spiritual journal of this pope, that his ideas on dialogue and on ecumenism were, in fact, very traditional and rather limited. The evidence seems quite convincing that in spite of personal sympathy for Orthodox and Protestant Christians, he never departed from the standard Catholic doctrine that the only acceptable kind of Christian unity was a return to Rome.

However, it is also true to say, with René Laurentin, that John XXIII was the personification of a certain spirit and that his secret strength was instinctual rather than intellectual. This strength was embodied in two basic laws which regulated his actions: the law of growth and the law of dialogue. Indeed, it is apparent that the notion of making Vatican II into a great step forward towards Christian unity was quite incidental to his original purpose in calling the council, and could be seen as almost accidental. In his journal he has described as 'entirely my own idea' the notion of a council, and at first this idea seemed to surprise even its author. In his opening allocution at the first session he said that it was 'completely unexpected, like a flash of heavenly light, shedding sweetness in eyes and hearts'. So, the possibility is that the Holy Spirit having sowed the seed of 'dialogue' in the twentieth century, allowed this Pope John, almost in spite of himself, to incorporate it into the Roman Catholic Church, much as his predecessor, John the evangelist, introduced the word 'logos' into the Fourth Gospel.

By June 1960 Pope John came to realize the importance of Christian unity as a public aim of the council even though this goal was still connected in his mind with reunion with Rome. However, once again, it was the intuition and the deed that really mattered and here again he furthered the intuitive cause which he was fostering by inviting Orthodox and Protestant observers to attend the council sessions and by setting up the Secretariat for Christian Unity. These gestures proved to be the seeds which caused the reality of ecumenical dialogue to flower in a way that surpassed the expectations of even the most visionary pioneers of this movement within the Roman Catholic Church.

So, the notion of 'dialogue' was greeted with euphoria by the world press and Pope John XXIII was projected through the media as the most open and the most popular pope that ever reigned in the see of Peter. Very little critical examination was applied either to the exact meaning of this word 'dialogue' in the vocabulary of the Pope himself or to its implications in Roman Catholic ecclesiology. In fact, Pope John XXIII died before any such detailed elucidation was either possible or necessary and this task became one of the more important preoccupations of his successor, Paul VI.

Jean Guitton in an article in the London *Tablet* of November 1963 made the following perceptive comment on both these popes. His remarks are all the more valuable since he was a personal friend of Pope Paul VI:

> John XXIII when he encountered serious difficulties raised himself above them by an act of supernatural faith; he surmounted them, he rose right above them, and so made them disappear. Paul VI, on the other hand, swoops on the difficulty like an eagle – he sees right through it, he feels it ... Paul VI likes to go to the heart of the matter and cause the solution to emerge from the core of the problem.

Many critics of the Roman Catholic Church since Vatican II have suggested that the notion of dialogue was a philosophical fashion which was borrowed in a misunderstood and cheapened form and incorporated into theological jargon to make the Church look relevant and attractive to a generation which prized the dimension of interpersonal human relationships. These critics would claim that the Church had exercised a somewhat typical sleight-of-hand whereby it pretended to be open and attentive to the insights of contemporary culture by paying lip-service to the current trends in popular philosophy, but that, in fact, its understanding and use of philosophical language, especially the term 'dialogue,' were misleading and detrimental both to the cause it sought to promote and the philosophy from which it claimed to be inspired.

In the context of such criticism, the names of Gabriel Marcel and Martin Buber are constantly evoked as sources from which the Church would have 'borrowed' its fashionable notion of dialogue. These two philosophers are hailed as the secular authors of this unprecedented term which appeared in the history of Roman Catholic theology for the first time in the documents of Vatican II. Pope John XXIII would be nominated as the unwitting carrier of this philosophy into the alien idiom of ecclesiastical terminology.

The implication here is that the notion of dialogue enjoyed intellectual respectability and rigorous scientific definition in the realm of philosophy from which it was drawn, and that it then faded into hazy liquidity and sentimentality when introduced into the more rarefied and eclectic setting of Roman Catholic doctrine. Such an evaluation of the problem is unjustified on two counts: it fails either to face up to the 'mystical' quality of the philosophical experience which gave birth to the notion of dialogue in the first place, or to do justice to the extremely rigorous examination of this concept undertaken by Paul VI.

Despite attempts to give a firm philosophical pedigree to 'dialogue' by linking it to the 'Copernican revolution' of modern thought, suggested by Feuerbach and elaborated by the so-called 'personalists', Gabriel Marcel had this to say about his own role in the introduction of this notion into the history of philosophy:[1]

> By a striking coincidence, I discovered the particular reality of the *Thou* at approximately the same time Buber was writing his book. His name was quite unknown to me…
>
> Thus we are faced with one of those cases of spiritual convergence which always merits attention. Generally they are not easy to interpret. Nevertheless, without calling directly upon that *Zeitgeist* which is always a little too easy to fall back on, we may say the following in this case:

At a time when a philosophy which concentrated more and more exclusively upon the world of the It, the denotable, upon the *Eswelt*, was leading into technocratic developments increasingly perilous for the integrity of man and even for his physical existence – the current atomic threat representing merely the paroxysm of this trend – it was surely inevitable that here and there men were moved to bring clearly and methodically to consciousness a counterpoise, that is, a consideration of the Thou.

And Martin Buber also admits that his 'philosophy' of dialogue was something given to him like a vision rather than something which he worked out for himself in a rigorously scientific fashion:[2]

> When I drafted the first sketch of this book (more than forty years ago). I was impelled by an inward necessity. A vision which had come to me again and again since my youth… had now reached steady clarity. This clarity was so manifestly suprapersonal in its nature that I at once knew I had to bear witness to it. Some time after I had received the right word as well and could write the book again in its final form, it became apparent that while there was need of some additions these had to be in their own place and in independent form.

And at the end of his life Buber wrote that 'no system was suitable for what I had to say. Structure was suitable for it, a compact structure but not one that joined everything together … It may not sacrifice to consistency anything of that reality which the experience that has happened commands it to point to.'[3] Later in the same final testament, at the end of his long life of dialogue, he concludes: 'I must say it again: I have no teaching, I only point to something. I point to reality. I point to something in reality that had not or had too little been seen. I take him who listens to me by the hand and lead him to the window. I open the window and point to what is outside'.[4]

Whatever these quotations may prove or disprove about the legitimacy of such intuitions in the history of philosophy proper, they certainly show that the origin of this notion of dialogue in the secular domain was no less abrupt and visionary than it was in the life of the Church. The vision which prompted John XXIII was similar to and as unformed as that shared contemporaneously by Buber and Marcel. In all three cases some suprapersonal intervention seems to have inspired the vision or the dream. And it has become a legend in the Vatican that when asked during an interview why he had decided to call a council together, Pope John XXIII went and opened a window in his study to illustrate the precise nature of that purpose.

The particular religious genius of John XXIII seems to have been his capacity to read what became incorporated into the Council documents in another ambiguous formula: 'the signs of the times'. He was able to detect and decipher what the Spirit was saying to the Churches in those ubiquitous manifestations of this presence in the world which cannot unfold themselves within the tight confines of the official ecclesiastical organism. These manifestations infiltrate their unprecedented and surprising directives through individual seers whose sensitivity and obediential capacity are subtle and sanguine enough to receive and to relay the vibrations without shock-absorbing distortion. John XXIII had the humility to know that the Spirit of God was alive and active in the world and that his task, as pope, was to listen to what that Spirit might by saying even to the Church of Rome itself.

The vision which this pope obeyed when summoning the second Vatican Council has much in common with the one which inspired both Buber and Marcel. It was based upon an experience which was authoritative and supralogical. Obviously reason is included in this experience, not as

autocratic judge or critic, but simply as one of the vehicles of
the experience. The task of explaining and elucidating the
experience is necessarily a logicizing one. Here reason becomes
the most important intermediary. However, it is important that
this task of elucidation be recognized as a second and derived
moment within the total experience. Buber puts this very
succinctly when describing the movement from initial vision to
philosophical elaboration in the case of his own notion of
'dialogue':[5]

> What is important, however, is that the indispensable
> capacity for thought not misjudge its office and act as if
> it were the authoritative recipient... It is incumbent upon
> it to logicize the superlogical, for which the law of
> contradiction does not hold valid; it is incumbent upon it
> to hold aloof from the inner contradiction; but it may
> not sacrifice to consistency anything of that reality itself
> which the experience that has happened commands it to
> point to.

This second task of elucidation of the vision of John XXIII, as
so often happens in an institution like the Roman Catholic
Church, fell to his successor, Paul VI, and, as again so often
happens in these cases, his gifts for logicizing and elaborating
rationally were vastly superior to those of his predecessor.
However, such gifts might have led him to misjudge his
function and his role, had he not been so aware of the visionary
quality of John XXIII's original intuition, and had he not had
himself so subtle an intellect.

Paul VI's elucidation of this concept came in his first
encyclical of 6 August 1964, published on the Feast of the
Transfiguration, *Ecclesiam Suam*. This text was a courageous
but ambiguous one: courageous because it faces up squarely to
the task of elaborating a mystery without allowing any of the
scope of that mystery to be lost in the consistency of the

elaboration; ambiguous because, in trying to elucidate the paradox which John XXIII's original vision encompassed, Paul VI is forced to stretch the grammar and the words he uses in logical presentation to the point where they, necessarily, cease to have the univocal clarity which a less opaque subject matter would both allow and require.

In a striking preamble, in which he compares the Church's dialogue with that dialogue which occurs between God and humanity, he stresses the inexpressible quality of all such dialogue:[6]

> Here then, Venerable Brethren, is the noble origin of this dialogue: in the mind of God himself. Religion of its very nature is a certain relationship between God and man. It finds its expression in prayer; and prayer is a dialogue. Revelation, too, that supernatural link which God has established with man, can likewise be looked upon as a dialogue... Indeed, the whole history of man's salvation is one long, varied dialogue, which marvelously begins with God and which he prolongs with men in so many different ways... Child and mystic, both are called to take part in this unfailing, trustful dialogue; and the mystic finds there the fullest scope for his spiritual powers.
>
> This relationship, this dialogue, which God the Father initiated and established with us through Christ in the Holy Spirit, is a very real one, even though it is difficult to express in words. We must examine it closely if we want to understand the relationship which we, the Church, should establish and foster with the human race.

However, after this preamble, he does go on to explain what kind of dialogue the Catholic Church can engage in and here all the ambiguity begins. This text, which predates the Vatican Council's Decree on Ecumenism, leaves us in doubt as to whether, at this point in time, Paul VI really recognizes the reality of other Christian denominations. Is not his notion of ecumenism no more than a disguised form of proselytism? Does it not really boil down to a programme of education towards a truth which his Church already possesses? He says explicitly in section 80 of the text that 'our dialogue presupposes that there exists in us a state of mind which we wish to communicate and foster in those around us'. Later in section 95 he says that what the Church is really saying to humankind is: 'Here in my possession is what you are looking for, what you need'. So, again we are left in doubt as to whether this version of ecumenical dialogue is no more than a repetition of the idea of Christian unity as a return to the fold. This becomes more probable, and more worrying to non-Catholic observers, at the end of the encyclical where (96) Paul VI sums up 'the situation' by describing it as a series of concentric circles around the central point at which God has placed the Roman Catholic Church. All other Christians seem to be defined according to their capacity to produce evidence of their similarity to the Church of Rome.

The Vatican Council's Decree on Ecumenism was promulgated on the 21 November 1964. This text represents a landmark in the history of Roman Catholic understanding of the notion of dialogue and although, at the time, it caused some disappointment to the more progressive among the Council fathers and to non-Catholic observers, it still contains an almost revolutionary step forward in Roman Catholic understanding of ecumenism.

Whatever appraisal one makes of the text itself, it becomes clear when one reads any official pronouncements that predate the Council, and the various debates which surround the wording of the final version, that the appearance of this text as an official conciliar document was almost miraculous. Certainly, most theologians would agree, it would never have been voted through by such an overwhelming majority of the council fathers if it had been proposed three years earlier.

From the very first words of the introduction which declares that 'the restoration of unity (*unitatis redintegratio*) among all Christians' is 'one of the principal concerns of the Second Vatican Council' a new tone is introduced into our dealings with other Churches. For the first time in her history, the Roman Catholic Church seems to envisage the unity of Christians in a light other than that of return to Rome and nowhere in this document do we find invitations to heretics and schismatics to repent of their ways. In fact, instead of the word 'schism', which was used in the past, this text uses the equally scriptural term 'divisions' to express the evils of disunity which are to be deplored in the one Church of Christ. There is also a healthy acceptance of blame for the initiation and maintenance of such divisions.

An important change took place in the heading for Chapter I of the text. The first proposal was 'Principles on Catholic Ecumenism'; this was changed in the final version to 'Catholic Principles on Ecumenism'. This may seem a small point, but, in fact, it represents an enormous shift of emphasis. It means that the Church no longer envisages ecumenism as something different for each of the various Churches. It sees it rather as a shared commitment and goal to which each of the partners in dialogue bring the principles of their own communion.

Such a distinction implies that the work of ecumenism is the work of the Holy Spirit, who is not confined in activity to the official channels of any one particular denomination. The Spirit's work in the field of ecumenism is seen, throughout this document, as something inspirational towards which all committed Christians are called. The document seeks to present the ecumenical movement in this light to 'all the Catholic faithful:'[7]

> Today, in many parts of the world, under the influence of
> the grace of the Holy Spirit, many efforts are being made
> in prayer, word and action to attain that fullness of unity

which Jesus Christ desires. The Sacred Council exhorts, therefore, all the Catholic faithful to recognize the signs of the times and to take an active and intelligent part in the work of ecumenism.

This text implies that the work of the Holy Spirit can, and does, realize itself outside the Catholic Church and that the members of this Church should be attentive to what this Spirit is saying to its members through 'the signs of the times' which are the explicit fruits of this unceasing presence of the Holy Spirit in our world. This recognition of other Churches as means for effecting grace is one of the most important intuitions expressed in this text. To measure the extent of this change both in tone and in approach towards ecumenical dialogue, we only have to quote a short passage from the encyclical of Pius XI, *Mortalium Animos*, where he deals with the same topic:[8]

There may be many non-Catholics who highly praise brotherly communion in Jesus Christ, but at the same time none of them is willing to submit himself to the magisterium and the pastoral office of the Vicar of Christ. They constantly emphasize that they would gladly discuss these matters with the Roman Catholic Church. But they want to carry on these discussions as equals having the same right. If such discussions should take place they would undoubtedly try to protect themselves through contractual understanding against the necessity of giving up those opinions which have forced them to this day to remain outside of the only sheepfold of Jesus Christ. Since this is the way things are, it is quite clear that the Apostolic See can under no circumstances take part in these meetings and that Roman Catholics are not permitted to favour such undertakings or to promote them. By participation they would merely increase the renown and the influence of the erring religions who are separated from the one Church established by Jesus Christ.

Twenty years later a number of Catholic theologians who wanted to participate as guests in the constituting convention of the World Council of Churches in Amsterdam in 1948 were forbidden by Rome to do so.

Thus, the revolutionary aspect of the Second Vatican Council's Decree on Ecumenism can only be measured against the official attitude of the Roman Catholic Church in the years which preceded it. From this point of view there can be no doubt about the extraordinary step forward in ecumenical dialogue which this historic text represents. As Yves Congar wrote in the preface to the Centurion edition of the Decree: 'The Decree on Ecumenism is more than a text, a teaching, a rule of behaviour or action; it is a 'deed' and this deed has bearings comparable to the great historical decisions that have decided the course of events for centuries afterwards'.

From the point of view of dialogue itself, the most important statement of the decree occurs in section 9:

> We must become familiar with the outlook of our separated brethren. Study is absolutely required for this, and it should be pursued in fidelity to the truth and with a spirit of good will. Catholics who already have a proper grounding need to acquire a more adequate understanding of the respective doctrines of our separated brethren, their history, their spiritual and liturgical life, their religious psychology and cultural background. Most valuable for this purpose are meetings of the two sides – especially for discussion of theological problems – where each can treat with the other on an equal footing, provided that those who take part in them under the guidance of the authorities are truly competent. From such dialogue will emerge still more

clearly what the situation of the Catholic Church really is. In this way, too, we will better understand the outlook of our separated brethren and more aptly present our own belief.

The two most interesting parts of this paragraph are the phrase 'on an equal footing' (*par cum pari*) which seemed to be a completely new understanding of this dialogue, but which, as Cardinal Jaeger pointed out in his book *A Stand on Ecumenism*,[9] is taken verbatim from the Instruction of the Holy Office 'On the Ecumenical Movement' of 20 December 1949, and the notion that 'from such dialogue' the situation of the Catholic Church will emerge. Originally the text read 'true position of the Catholic communion' but, at the suggestion of one father, this was changed to 'true position of the Catholic Church'. This last phrase could be interpreted in either of two ways. It could mean that dialogue would lead others to a real understanding of the truth already contained within the Catholic Church, or it could mean that the true situation of the Catholic Church would emerge as a result of such dialogue. Both these notions are instances of the ambiguity of the Council document and its openness towards interpretation in several different ways, according to the particular bias of the reader.

Finally, the most noteworthy change of emphasis which occurs in this document concerns the Catholic Church's understanding of herself in the context of ecumenical dialogue. Far from regarding Rome as the *princeps analogans* from which all other Churches are required to chart their identity, which was the impression given by *Ecclesiam Suam*, the text here seems to suggest another criterion in the form of proximity to the Gospel norm, which is seen as a common law in function of which even the Church must seek to reform herself. The final paragraph of the decree deserves to be quoted in full:

This sacred Council firmly hopes that the initiative of the sons of the Catholic Church, joined with those of the separated brethren, will go forward, without obstructing the ways of divine Providence, and without pre-judging the future inspirations of the Holy Spirit. Further, this Council declares that it realizes that this holy objective – the reconciliation of all Christians in the unity of the one and only Church of Christ – transcends human powers and gifts. It therefore places its hope entirely in the prayer of Christ for the Church, in the love of the Father for us, and in the power of the Holy Spirit. 'And hope does not disappoint, because God's love has been poured forth in our hearts through the Holy Spirit who has been given to us' (Rom. 5:5)

An impression was given by the popular press, at the time of the promulgation of the Decree on Ecumenism by the Second Vatican Council, that an autocratic intervention was made at the last minute by Pope Paul VI which drastically changed both the tone and the content of this document. This impression later developed into a myth, whereby the spirit of ecumenism within the Catholic Church was stifled at birth by a conservative minority who managed to persuade Pope Paul VI to radically change the decree such that it made it possible for the Roman Curia later to interpret this document in a way that brought this whole movement to a standstill.

This mythology is based on a certain number of facts, a serious misinterpretation of these facts, and a great deal of wishful thinking. It is true that the schema 'On Ecumenism' was worked out chiefly by Belgian, French and Dutch theologians and that a minority of the Fathers and theologians from other countries were opposed to it. It is also true that although there was an overwhelming majority of votes for the second version of the schema, there were 1069 votes *iuxta modum* in the cases of the first three chapters of the decree.

These reservations or suggestions for alterations were delivered in writing to the general secretariat of the Council on the day of voting or on the following day. This resulted in almost two thousand *modi* or suggestions for alterations for these three chapters of the schema. The General Secretariat of the Council turned over all these *modi* to the Secretariat for Christian Unity. After working through these suggestions, this Secretariat made twenty-nine emendations to the text, but none of these changed either the content or the spirit of the schema; rather they clarified it and prevented misunderstandings.

The result of this work by the Secretariat for Unity was presented to the Council Fathers in three printed volumes comprising a hundred pages each. The outcome of all this showed that a small minority were still convinced that insufficient attention had been paid to their objections. These felt that a petition to the Pope was the only way to obtain a further hearing for their persistent misgivings. On 19 November 1964, the Secretary General of the Council announced that the final vote on the schema 'On Ecumenism' would take place the following day. He then read the nineteen corrections which were to be inserted into the text, introducing these as follows: 'Apart from the corrections already inserted, which had been accepted by the Council Fathers on the basis of the *modi*, the following have been added by the Secretariat for Unity in order to make the text clearer. In this way the Secretariat has accepted benevolent suggestions that had been authoritatively expressed'.

This preamble allowed the popular press to suggest that the Pope had simply forced these alterations upon the Fathers of the Council. What actually happened was that the minority petition had been submitted to the Pope between Saturday, 14 November 1964, and Wednesday, 18 November, when he sent forty suggestions for alteration to the Secretariat for Unity. This Secretariat, in the short time allowed them before the vote was taken on the decree, accepted just under half the alterations sent to them, considering that the content and general tenor of the decree would not be affected by them.

The next day, Thursday 19 November, which came to be known by some as 'Black Thursday', was a particularly frustrating one for the Council Fathers, because it was the day when they learned that the vote which was supposed to be taken on the Declaration 'On Religious Liberty' would have to be postponed until the next session. This announcement caused a great deal of disappointment and consternation as well as much speculation about the reasons for such a decision. When, on top of this, the nineteen alterations to the text 'On Ecumenism' were also revealed for the first time at this same session, the atmosphere within the Council became, understandably, tense.

In fact, the chief enemy in both these cases was the shortage of time and the ensuing impossibility of adequate and comprehensive information and explanation being supplied to the general body. The onus fell upon Pope Paul VI to guide the Council through these very frustrating last days. With hindsight, it can be seen that he fulfilled this task with discretion, courage and foresight, even though, at the time, his actions may have been interpreted as arbitrary and autocratic.

In the case of the postponement of the vote on the Declaration on Religious Liberty, the completely revised text of this schema had only been distributed to the Council Fathers on 17 November, two days before the scheduled date of the final vote. An appreciable minority complained to the Council authorities that such procedures contravened Article 30, 2 of the *Ordo Concilii Vaticani II Celebrandi,* which stipulates that a suitable period of time must be allowed between the distribution of the revised text and the final vote, to permit the Fathers to reach a mature judgement on the way they should vote. Such time was simply not available under the circumstances and this situation was compounded by the fact that the new text in its totality of 556 lines contained only seventy-five lines of the earlier one, which it claimed to have 'revised'. Under these circumstances and as a result of the minority petition, the presiding Council decided that, on the basis of Article 30, 2 of the Council's Ordo, they had no choice but to postpone this vote.

Quite understandably, this caused frustration among the majority of the Council Fathers, causing 441 of them to present a written petition to the Pope asking him to allow the vote to proceed as planned. The Pope referred this petition to the supervisory court of the Council, which ruled that if this petition were granted it would deny the explicit rights of the minority as laid down in the Council's Ordo. Under these circumstances, there was really no decision possible for the Pope to take other than that of accepting the ruling of the supervisory court in this case.

After such a decision, it is understandable also that the atmosphere in the Council hall was hardly favourable towards the introduction of the nineteen alternations into the text 'On Ecumenism' and this goes a long way towards accounting for the many bitter words of disillusionment which were later seized upon and magnified by the popular press, hungry as always for some sensational news. Credit must be given to such discerning newspapers as *Le Monde* which resisted the temptation to sensationalize and reported in a perspicacious article of 25 November, 1964:

> A pope is first and foremost an arbiter. Paul VI is so determined to fulfil this duty that he has not hesitated to risk being misunderstood either by a majority or by a minority.

In the final analysis it becomes clear that the suggestion that the document on ecumenism was qualitatively altered and disfigured by an autocratic intervention at the last moment by Paul VI at the insistent prompting of a minority of conservatives, is false at three important levels.

The first is a misunderstanding of the intervention and the role of a pope in such circumstances. The idea that a Church Council is a democratic forum where the vote of a majority should always hold sway is false. Respect must be shown for the voice of a minority which conscientiously objects to any particular aspect of the text under discussion. The criterion of judgement here is not simply the number of votes in favour, it is a much more subtle one of discerning the truth and trying to lead the Council Fathers towards a consensus which would leave no doubt about the intrinsic validity of the decisions finally taken. The role of a pope in such circumstances is to ensure that proper procedure is followed and that the rights of every member of the Council are fully respected.

The second is a failure to recognize the existence of a distinct structure and order or procedure which are independent of the rights of a minority or of a majority within the Council itself, or of the intervention of papal authority within the framework of the Council's schedule. The *Ordo Concillii Vaticani II Celebrandi* is an objective court of appeal which can be called upon by any number of individual members of the Council whenever they feel that their rights are not being respected or that the correct order and method for conducting the Council's business is being flouted.

The third is an overestimation of any Church document and unrealistic expectations at the level of ecumenical dialogue. Those who had allowed themselves to hope for unprecedented and miraculous advances towards the unity of Christendom had to vent their inevitable disappointment with the somewhat cautious and banal text that eventually issued from the Council Fathers, by supposing that the utopian ideal that they had hoped for must have been sabotaged along the way by the malevolent intervention of evil forces.

In fact, the final text, as promulgated on 21 November 1964, despite the regrettable psychological effects produced by the last minute changes, was in no way fundamentally altered. It does represent very accurately the advances made by the Roman Catholic Church in this rather vexed area and, when read carefully in the context of the history which preceded it and the debates which brought it about, should be recognized as a very significant step forward. The only effect of the nineteen modifications was to have made the text, if anything, more ambiguous, and, in the light of what came afterwards, this may have been inevitable.

We have the testimony of Yves Congar, one of the theologians who was most influential in the promotion of this cause, that the final text in no way alters fundamentally the spirit of what was originally proposed. In his introduction to the Centurion edition of the Council Document he says:

> After another careful reading of the three chapters 'On Ecumenism' I can say in all truthfulness that their content and general purport remains unchanged. Any person reading them for the first time, and knowing nothing of the episode just recounted, would see nothing other than a candid, forthright declaration of the ecumenical attitude of a unanimous Catholic Church with the pope at its head. The text has certainly not been watered down. Three years ago none of us would have thought that it would meet with unanimous agreement in its present form. But we have no wish to influence anyone's mind in advance. We shall only say, like the voice which Augustine heard in the garden at Milan, *'Tolle, lege'* – take and read. The text will speak for itself.

In the same introduction Congar also says that:

> The decree expresses the mind of John XXIII, who, even though he did not write a single line of it, may be considered its spiritual author. Indeed, John XXIII wanted the Council, and set before it two aims which he saw as

very closely related to one another: the inner renewal of the Church and the work of Christian reunion.

Response to the text of the decree on Ecumenism was, on the whole, generous and optimistic. Most people saw it as a positive step forward, but felt that the fruits it might bear would depend upon the way in which it was interpreted and the direction that the official Catholic Church would take after the Council. Such reaction was perhaps best summed up in the report made by the observer delegated by the World Council of Churches to the Council, Dr Lukas Vischer:[10]

> The results reflect the image of Jesus, the God of two faces and the protector of doors and entrances. On the one hand, they open the door not only to a renewal in depth, but also to a more profound communion with the Churches separated from Rome. On the other hand, they continue the tradition specific to the Roman Catholic Church; they represent an adaptation of the old Roman Catholic position of this modern age, a transposition in a modern context. All will depend, therefore, on the way in which the texts will be interpreted in the years to come, for ultimately Rome will have to decide which face she intends to present and then bury the other.

Three possible interpretations of ecumenical dialogue seem to have been detected by different observers in their reading of this text.

The first would believe that the Roman Church has now done all that could be done in terms of inner renewal and reconciliation. After this Council, the Roman Church is a renewed and fully Catholic Church that is ready to give of her riches to those who lack them. The document 'On Ecumenism' is an open invitation to Christian unity, which is thereby envisaged as a return to this renewed and reconciliatory Roman Church.

The second would look upon this Decree as a beginning. This would imply that the renewal of the Church is still to come. Thus the call to reunion is not a call to 'return', but to 'reconciliation', which would be accomplished by a change of heart in all the Christian Churches achieved through dialogue between the separated brethren.

The third would avoid any dogmatically or canonically fixed conception of unity. It would suggest that there are theologians and lay people within the Roman Catholic Church who are less definite in their understanding of future Christian unity and are completely open to the working of the Holy Spirit. In this view it seems possible that changes will take place within the structure and the teaching of the Roman Church which would allow a kind of unity to emerge and would result from a mutual giving and taking among the different Churches engaged in dialogue on an equal footing.

It is probable that many combinations of these three interpretations inspired the fathers who voted in the Council for the decree. Neither the motivation nor the possible interpretations are as important as the actual text itself. This text left many commentators with the impression that, although a step forward had been taken, the Roman Catholic Church had not yet crossed the threshold of genuine ecumenical dialogue. Such was the opinion, for instance, of Fr Maurice Villain, a Roman Catholic expert on ecumenism at the Council, who declared in *Rhythmes du Monde* in 1964:[11]

> This schema is not really ecumenical. This complaint was voiced by all the observers that I consulted and I associate myself entirely with this point of view. The Roman Catholic Church speaks here of ecumenism from the point of view of itself considered as the centre and judging all other Churches and communities in comparison with its own fullness, I was almost going to say 'totalitarianism', judging them quantitatively and not

qualitatively. In other words, each separated community is measured according to the number of Roman Catholic elements which it has retained or jettisoned. Such an attitude is quite inaccurate, not to say entirely false. In fact, each Christian community has its own particular axis of vision and structure, not with reference to the Roman Church, but to the Revelation of Jesus Christ, as each one understands it; each one is very much more than just a lesser or watered down version of Catholicism. Even in those paragraphs which are skillfully worked and considerate towards the Oriental Churches, these latter, according to professor Nissiotis, fail completely to recognize themselves.

The legacy of the Decree on Ecumenism to the post-conciliar Church could almost be described as three irreconcilable and almost antagonistic axioms which had to be combined in however paradoxical a form to encompass the full reality of 'Ecumenical Dialogue'.

The first of these axioms is that 'The Catholic participant, believing as he does that the Lord has confided to the Catholic Church the fullness of the means of salvation and all truth revealed by God, will be ready to give an account of his faith'.[12] The second axiom concerns the dialogue itself: 'Ecumenical dialogue will be conducted between the participants as between equals. Everything that has been said about the nature, aim and bases of this dialogue, notably concerning reciprocity and mutual commitment, provides a basis for this attitude of equality'.[13] The third is the conviction that this very notion of 'dialogue' is something new ('an important modern phenomenon, the development of dialogue in the modern world, and especially among Christians'[14]) which does not come out of the Catholic Church, but from the 'modern world', to which the Roman Catholic Church has been called by the Holy Spirit. This means that the Church must be careful to 'go forward without obstructing the ways of divine Providence and without prejudging the future inspiration of the Holy Spirit'.[15]

Now it is almost incontrovertibly clear that, within the framework of most known epistemologies, the first of these axioms makes the second impossible to hold and the third has precisely the same effect upon the first. And yet, since Vatican II, the attempt of most theologians in this sphere has been to juggle these three axioms in such a way that the illusion is being given that all three are being fundamentally respected.

In all these explanations of dialogue there seems to be agreement that this reality constitutes either an action or an attitude of the Church, rather than an expression of its being. As there have always been two fundamental aspects of the life of the Church, the *ecclesia docens* and the *ecclesia discens*, the way in which the new reality of dialogue would become incorporated into Church life must assume either of these two modalities. It would become either the dialogue of an apostle or the dialogue of a disciple. The first would be the discerning and compassionate dialogue of education; the second would be the open and humble dialogue of equality.

Both schools of thought would detect a fundamental difference between the teaching of Vatican II contained in the Decree on Ecumenism and the encyclical of Paul VI *Ecclesiam Suam*. The first group would regard the papal document as a definitive exegesis of the later conciliar text and would reinforce this theory by quoting the first encyclical of John Paul II, *Redemptor Hominis* issued on 4 March 1979, in which he defines 'dialogue' in terms of the first encyclical of his predecessor:[16]

> The Church's consciousness must go with universal openness, in order that all may be able to find in her 'the unsearchable riches of Christ' spoken of by the Apostle to the Gentiles. Such openness, organically joined with the awareness of her own nature and certainty of her

own truth... is what gives the Church her apostolic, or in other words her missionary, dynamism, professing and proclaiming in its integrity the whole of the truth transmitted by Christ. At the same time she must carry on the dialogue that Paul VI, in his Encyclical *Ecclesiam Suam* called 'the dialogue of salvation', distinguishing with precision the various circles within which it was to be carried on.

The second group would hold that the notion of dialogue contained in the Decree on Ecumenism was a qualitative advance on the definition given by Paul VI in his earlier encyclical. They would claim that Paul VI himself recognized this advance under the impulse of the Holy Spirit and, after the council, was led to modify some of the views expressed in the earlier encyclical. In support of this theory, the *ecclesia discens* school of thought would quote two important sources. The first is an address given by Paul VI on 28 April 1967, to the full assembly of the Secretariat for Unity, in which he says:[17]

> The Council has placed an obligation upon us and has marked out the way forward: the council documents, which either explicitly or implicitly treat of the question of the reintegration (recomposition) of the unity of the unique Church by all those who bear the name of Christians, are so authoritative and so explicit and having such a dynamism of orientation and obligation, that they offer to Catholic ecumenism a doctrinal and pastoral basis which it never had before.
>
> We would have to admit that we are here faced with a fact, in which the Holy Spirit, who guides and animates the Church, played the principal and determining part. We shall be both faithful and docile to this Spirit.

The second is a conversation about the precise meaning of dialogue between Pope Paul VI and his friend and admirer, the theologian, Jean Guitton, in which the Pope explains his thoughts on dialogue in terms of its foundation in love and the equality of its partners in terms of 'an equal love of truth'.[18]

Whatever may be said about the accuracy of these interpretations, it is clear that what we lack is a genuine theology of ecumenical dialogue and, above all, an official theology of such dialogue. The 'Reflections and suggestions concerning Ecumenical Dialogue' issued by the Secretariat for the Promotion of the Unity of Christians in September 1970 were a brave and humble attempt to present guidelines, without trying to be normative in this difficult, new and vexed area. The document says of itself that it 'does not have strict juridical authority' that its 'authority resides uniquely in the fact that it is the result of prolonged reflection made on many levels by those engaged in ecumenical dialogue'. The result is a neatly balanced attempt to hold together the three axioms quoted above with several sprinklings of quotations from 'A working paper on Ecumenical Dialogue' prepared by the Joint Working Group between the World Council of Churches and the Roman Catholic Church (1967). This combination produces a paradoxical sequence of paragraphs which seem to contradict each other:[19]

> Ecumenical dialogue ... aims at preparing the way for their unity of faith in the bosom of a Church one and visible ... This unity, we believe, dwells in the Catholic Church as something she can never lose, and we hope that it will continue to increase until the end of time ... That unity is the ultimate aim of the thoughts and desires of those engaged in dialogue, who are preparing themselves to receive it as the great gift that God alone will bestow, in the way and at the time that he wishes.

Now, this passage contains all the ambiguity which has dogged most Catholic statements about ecumenical dialogue. It could mean that the Roman Catholic Church contains the full truth and unity of the Church of Christ and that all Christians of good will are secretly longing for that unity and truth, but that their understanding of this secret is still faulty and that God, in his own way and in his own good time, will, through dialogue, bring them to this realization and they will become absorbed in that fullness of unity and truth.

Or it could mean that, despite the fact that the Roman Catholic Church has to go on maintaining the fact that she already possesses both the unity and the truth which ecumenical dialogue is all about, if she continues to actively engage in such dialogue with other Christians of good will, she, and all the other partners in dialogue, will be led, in spite of themselves, to that unique unity which God alone knows and has planned for the one Church of Christ.

Notes

1   Gabriel Marcel, 'I and Thou' in *The Philosophy of Martin Buber* (London & Illinois, 1967), pp. 41-48.

2   Martin Buber, *I and Thou,* translated by Ronald Gregor Smith (Edition with Postscript added, New York, 1960), p. 123.

3   *The Philosophy of Martin Buber* (London & Illinois, 1967), p. 690.

4   Ibid., p. 693.

5   Ibid., p. 690.

6   *Ecclesiam Suam,* paragraphs 70 & 71.

7   *Vatican Council II, The Conciliar and Post Conciliar Documents*, edited by Austin Flannery, OP (Dublin, 1980), p. 545.

8   Encyclical Letter of Pope Pius XI, *Mortalium Animos*, 1928.

9   Lorenz Cardinal Jaeger, *A Stand on Ecumenism: The Council's Decree* (London, 1965), p. 110.

10   Reported in *Concilium* April 1966, vol. 4 no. 2, p. 66. I am sure that the original report must have used the god Janus, rather than Jesus, but I quote as it is printed in the source available to me.

11   Reported in *Rhythmes du Monde*, 1964, XII, 1, p. 56.

12   'Reflections and Suggestions Concerning Ecumenical Dialogue' issued by the Secretariat for the Promotion of the Unity of

Christians in September 1970 (*Vatican Council II*, Flannery 1981 edition), p. 543, no. 2a.

13   Ibid., p. 542, no. 2.

14   Ibid., p. 537.

15   Ibid., p. 539.

16   Encyclical Letter of Pope John Paul II, *Redemptor Hominis*, 4, 1979.

17   Text provided in *Irenikon*, 1967, no. 2.

18   Jean Guitton, *The Pope Speaks* (London, 1968), p. 167.

19   As in note 13, Section II, 2: 'Nature & aim of Ecumenical Dialogue'.

CHAPTER II

FROM POPE JOHN PAUL II TO THE NEW MILLENNIUM

Pope John Paul II not only encouraged and promoted the thirteen different ecumenical dialogues in which the Roman Catholic Church had been engaged, but he regards his pontificate as an essentially ecumenical one. The word *'pontifex'* in Latin means a builder of bridges and that is how John Paul II has seen himself during the twenty-five years of his pontificate. Visits he made to Egypt, Mount Sinai, Greece, Syria, Ukraine and Armenia were explicitly ecumenical in intent. It is no secret that he was disappointed when the year 2000 did not bring Catholic-Orthodox relations to the point of unity 'around the altar of concelebration', which would have meant the Church was again permitted to 'breathe with the two lungs' of East and West. However, others would see this ambition as an urge towards monarchy and monopoly which would make the Roman Catholic Church into a monolithic inevitability to which all other Christians must eventually adhere. Pope John Paul II might deny any such totalitarian ambition.

There is no doubt that when he took office the ecumenical movement was in the doldrums. The 1994 Common Christological Declaration between the Roman Catholic Church and the Assyrian Church of the East, solving difficulties dating back to Nestorius, and the 1999 Joint Declaration of the Catholic Church and the Lutheran World Federation on the doctrine of justification, were triumphs which allowed him to present himself as one who breathed new life into a dying movement. His views on dialogue can be found most elaborately in his Encyclical 'That They May Be One' 25 May 1995[1] where he describes the fruits of such dialogue in terms of 'brotherhood rediscovered [41].'

This encyclical reiterates emphatically that: 'at the Second Vatican Council, the Catholic Church committed herself *irrevocably* to following the path of the ecumenical venture, thus heeding the Spirit of the Lord, who teaches people to interpret carefully the "signs of the times [#3]."' This commitment is, therefore, not linked to an apostolic imperative internal to the Roman Catholic Church, but rather to the ubiquitous and untrammelled inspiration of the Holy Spirit in the wider context of the contemporary history of the whole world. A council document provides the authority which eliminates the suggestion of mere proselytising evangelism as motivation for Roman Catholic ecumenism. The unity of ecumenism is not imposed from without, it establishes itself 'by virtue of its own truth, as it makes its entrance into the mind at once quietly and with power.'[2] In this argument the Pope was probably thinking of places where Catholicism is not only starved of dialogue, but is also deprived of the right to exist. He insists that the Church 'seeks nothing for herself but the freedom to proclaim the Gospel. Indeed, her authority is exercised in the service of truth and charity'. Truth and love are universals which predate and transcend any of the Christian denominations and are the realities upon which Christian dialogue are based. He commits himself energetically to this task:

> I myself intend to promote every suitable initiative aimed at making the witness of the entire Catholic

community understood in its full purity and consistency, especially considering the engagement which awaits the Church at the threshold of the new Millennium. That will be an exceptional occasion, in view of which she asks the Lord to increase the unity of all Christians until they reach full communion.[3] The present Encyclical Letter is meant as a contribution to this most noble goal. Essentially pastoral in character, it seeks to encourage the efforts of all who work for the cause of unity.

In # 4 he suggests that 'in our ecumenical age, marked by the Second Vatican Council, the mission of the Bishop of Rome is particularly directed to recalling the need for full communion among Christ's disciples'. The Catholic Church is, by definition, committed to the cause of unity. Ecumenism, in some perhaps as yet unclear understanding of this term, is part and parcel of what Catholicism means constitutionally. However, even though John Paul II agrees that the eventual unity which all Christians must embrace is a gift of the Holy Spirit, he is still quite clear what that unity must entail. This means that although the source of unity is a divine gift, the result is a foreseeable assembly for which he already has the blueprint. This is stated most clearly in # 9:

> In effect, this unity bestowed by the Holy Spirit does not merely consist in the gathering of people as a collection of individuals. It is a unity constituted by the bonds of the profession of faith, the sacraments and hierarchical *communion*.[4] The faithful are one because, in the Spirit, they are in *communion* with the Son and, in him, share in his communion with the Father: 'Our *fellowship* is with the Father and with his Son Jesus Christ' (1 Jn. 1:3). For the Catholic Church, then, the communion of Christians is none other than the manifestation in them of the grace by which God makes them sharers in his own *communion*,

which is his eternal life. Christ's words 'that they may be one' are thus his prayer to the Father that the Father's plan may be fully accomplished, in such a way that everyone may clearly see 'what is the plan of the mystery hidden for ages in God who created all things' (Eph. 3:9). To believe in Christ means to desire unity; to desire unity means to desire the Church; to desire the Church means to desire the communion of grace which corresponds to the Father's plan from all eternity. Such is the meaning of Christ's prayer: *'Ut unum sint'*.

So far, so good. There could hardly be a Christian who reads the Gospels who would not agree with such a definition of Christian unity. However in the next paragraph [#10] where the realization of this unity here on earth begins to take shape, we enter less obvious territory:

The Second Vatican Council strengthened this commitment with a clear ecclesiological vision, open to all the ecclesial values present among other Christians. The Council states that the Church of Christ 'subsists in the Catholic Church, which is governed by the Successor of Peter and by the Bishops in communion with him', and at the same time acknowledges that 'many elements of sanctification and of truth can be found outside her visible structure.'

The ambiguity again centres on the understanding of the word 'subsists'. It does not mean for this pope that the Church of Christ exists in the Roman Catholic Church exclusively. He accepts the council teaching that the Holy Spirit can and does infuse other Churches. 'It follows that these separated Churches and Communities, though we believe that they suffer from defects, have by no means been deprived of significance and value in the mystery of salvation. For the Spirit of Christ has not refrained from using them as means of salvation which derive their efficacy from the very fullness of grace and truth entrusted to the Catholic Church' [#12]. However, he interprets this with his own slant which suggests that whatever percentage of the true spirit of Christ may be present in separated Churches is geared towards recognition of and return to the one Church of Christ. 'These elements, however, as gifts properly belonging to the Church of Christ, possess an inner dynamism towards Catholic unity' [#11]. Again, the reader is left wondering whether this 'Catholic unity' is something which already exists in the Church of Rome or whether it is something which all the disparate elements of Christian inspiration will unite to form at some future date. This second interpretation is unlikely, given the profile of the Roman Catholic Church in the same paragraph [#11]:

> The Catholic Church thus affirms that during the two thousand years of her history she has been preserved in unity, with all the means with which God wishes to endow his Church, and this despite the often grave crises which have shaken her, the infidelity of some of her ministers, and the faults into which her members daily fall. The Catholic Church knows that, by virtue of the strength which comes to her from the Spirit, the weaknesses, mediocrity, sins and at times the betrayals of some of her children cannot destroy what God has bestowed on her as part of his plan of grace. Moreover, 'the powers of death shall not prevail against it' (Mt. 16:18).

There is a welcome reiteration of the responsibility acknowledged for sins against unity: 'Even so, the Catholic Church does not forget that many among her members cause God's plan to be discernible only with difficulty'. More than this, the Pope acknowledges that his Church was one of the causes of disunity. Again he quotes the Decree on Ecumenism to the effect that 'people of both sides were to blame' [#13] so that responsibility cannot be attributed only to the 'other side'. By God's grace, however, he claims that, despite such universal sins against unity, 'neither what belongs to the structure of the Church of Christ nor that communion which still exists with the other Churches and Ecclesial Communities has been destroyed'. The Golden Bowl of that original Church of Christ may have been cracked and disfigured but it is still recognizably present on earth, which also explains why some of it is present in the separated Churches:

> Indeed, the elements of sanctification and truth present in the other Christian Communities, in a degree which varies from one to the other, constitute the objective basis of the communion, albeit imperfect, which exists between them and the Catholic Church.
>
> To the extent that these elements are found in other Christian Communities, the one Church of Christ is effectively present in them. For this reason the Second Vatican Council speaks of a certain, though imperfect communion. The Dogmatic Constitution *Lumen Gentium* stresses that the Catholic Church 'recognizes that in many ways she is linked' [#14] with these Communities by a true union in the Holy Spirit.

#12 lists comprehensively 'the elements of sanctification and truth' which in various ways are present and operative beyond the visible boundaries of the Catholic Church: Sacred Scripture, of course, takes pride of place. But it is also true that in many cases these Christians are 'consecrated by Baptism, through which they are united with Christ'.

> They also recognize and receive other sacraments within their own Churches or Ecclesial Communities. Many of

them rejoice in the episcopate, celebrate the Holy Eucharist, and cultivate devotion towards the Virgin Mother of God. They also share with us in prayer and other spiritual benefits. Likewise, we can say that in some real way they are joined with us in the Holy Spirit, for to them also he gives his gifts and graces, and is thereby operative among them with his sanctifying power. Some indeed he has strengthened to the extent of the shedding of their blood. In all of Christ's disciples the Spirit arouses the desire to be peacefully united, in the manner determined by Christ, as one flock under one shepherd' [#15].

Then begins the distribution of prizes to those who are nearest to the Roman Catholic Church. John Paul II, with his manifest predilection for the Orthodox believers, reminds us that 'the Council's Decree on Ecumenism, referring to the Orthodox Churches, went so far as to declare that "through the celebration of the Eucharist of the Lord in each of these Churches, the Church of God is built up and grows in stature" [#16]. Truth demands that all this be recognized'. So 'Truth' is the absolute category from which individual Churches are assessed and situated in their relative distances from the already existing one true Church. However, as # 14 clarifies:

It is not a matter of adding together all the riches scattered throughout the various Christian Communities in order to arrive at a Church which God has in mind for the future. In accordance with the great Tradition, attested to by the Fathers of the East and of the West, the Catholic Church believes that in the Pentecost Event God has *already* manifested the Church in her eschatological reality, which he had prepared 'from the time of Abel, the just one'. [#19] This reality is something already given. Consequently we are even now in the last times. The elements of this already-given Church exist, found in their fullness in the Catholic Church and, without this fullness, in the other Communities, [#20] where certain features of the Christian mystery have at times been more effectively emphasized. Ecumenism is directed precisely to making the partial communion existing between Christians grow towards full communion in truth and charity.

#15 quotes: *'There can be no ecumenism worthy of the name without a change of heart'*. [#21] Both the Council and the Pope call for personal conversion as well as for communal conversion and this, presumably applies to all Christians of whatever denomination. Apart from the 'Truth' as monitor of one's claim to authenticity as the Church of Christ, there is also the objective norm of the Scriptures. The Pope recognises that 'the desire of every Christian Community for unity goes hand in hand with its fidelity to the Gospel'.

So we again find ourselves wandering through a fog of ambiguity. When in #16 we are told that 'by engaging in frank dialogue, Communities help one another to look at themselves together in the light of the Apostolic Tradition' does this include the Roman Catholic Church in the same way as all the other 'communities'? And if so, does such dialogue lead them 'to ask themselves whether they truly express in an adequate way all that the Holy Spirit has transmitted through the Apostles'? [#24] And does this imply self-examination which might mean transformation of the ecclesiastical structures as presently known and implemented?

Even after the many sins which have contributed to our historical divisions, *Christian unity is possible*, provided that we are humbly conscious of having sinned against unity and are convinced of our need for conversion. Not only personal sins must be forgiven and left behind, but also social sins, which is to say the sinful 'structures' themselves which have contributed and can still contribute to division and to the reinforcing of division.

Does this last paragraph apply to the Roman Catholic Church and its structures also? Does it mean that every one of us stands equally in the dock awaiting judgement from the one Lord about the extent of our fidelity to His explicit commands? A later section refers to such a 'vertical' dimension to any Christian dialogue:

> Dialogue cannot take place merely on a horizontal level, being restricted to meetings, exchanges of points of view or even the sharing of gifts proper to each Community. It has also a primarily vertical thrust, directed towards the One who, as the Redeemer of the world and the Lord of history, is himself our Reconciliation. This vertical aspect of dialogue lies in our acknowledgment, jointly and to each other, that we are men and women who have sinned. It is precisely this acknowledgment which creates in brothers and sisters living in Communities not in full communion with one another that interior space where Christ, the source of the Church's unity, can effectively act, with all the power of his Spirit, the Paraclete [#35].

#26 almost provides hope that ecumenism might mean establishing the unity of Christianity through a Church quite unrecognisable in form and structure from any that exists today:

> 'Ecumenical' prayer, as the prayer of brothers and sisters, expresses all this. Precisely because they are separated from one another, they meet in Christ with all the more hope, *entrusting to him the future of their unity and their*

communion. Here too we can appropriately apply the teaching of the Council: 'The Lord Jesus, when he prayed to the Father *"that all may be one . . . as we are one"* (Jn. 17:21-22), opened up vistas closed to human reason. For he implied a certain likeness between the union of the Divine Persons, and the union of God's children in truth and charity.' [48]

The last three lines of this last quotation suggest that the unity that we search for as Christians is the kind of relationship that exists between the three persons of the Trinity. It allows for communion between different persons each of whom are really distinct though equal. Dialogue between Christians is a similar conversation in depth. Later in this encyclical a specific heading is given to 'ecumenical dialogue' where [# 28] prayer is recognized as the 'soul' of ecumenical renewal and of the yearning for unity, and dialogue is linked to trends in contemporary 'personalist' philosophy, where the Pope himself is usually catalogued as a thinker:

[Prayer] is the basis and support for *everything the Council defines as 'dialogue'.* This definition is certainly not unrelated to today's *personalist way of thinking.* The capacity for 'dialogue' is rooted in the nature of the person and his dignity. As seen by philosophy, this approach is linked to the Christian truth concerning man as expressed by the Council: man is in fact 'the only creature on earth which God willed for itself'; thus he cannot 'fully find himself except through a sincere gift of himself'. [51] Dialogue is an indispensable step along the path *towards human self-realization,* the self-realization both of *each individual* and *of every human community.* Although the concept of 'dialogue' might appear to give priority to the cognitive dimension (*dia-logos*), all dialogue implies a global, existential dimension. It involves the human subject in his or her entirety; dialogue between communities involves in a particular way the subjectivity of each.

Every line of this last quotation is brim full of possibility. The whole paragraph is fertile ground for an understanding of dialogue as something essentially human, unambiguously mandatory for everyone, and comprehensively universal, excluding no member of the human race. The 'global, existential dimension' implies a universal ontological birthright. The fact of being born makes me a partner in dialogue. 'Dialogue is an indispensable step along the path *towards human self-realization*'. Each of these sentences requires elucidation. This will involve both the personalist philosophy of John Paul II himself, but also some contemporary philosophical viewpoint. This latter will be provided in the next chapter on Martin Buber. In summary, however, it is as if the Pope is saying that as persons we *are* a dialogue. No person can off-load this reality. It is 'existential', it is part of what we are as human persons. Christology is 'deficient anthropology' in the words of Karl Rahner. It is the realization of what we already are. It is also a reminder of what we are called to become. Being in dialogue is stepping into the essential space of personhood.

However, a later reference to *Ecclesiam Suam* seems to suggest that this previous encyclical of Paul VI is both the source of the later Council document on Ecumenism, and John Paul II's elaboration here. At the same time he interprets all three as understanding dialogue as gift of the Holy Spirit:

> This truth about dialogue, so profoundly expressed by Pope Paul VI in his Encyclical *Ecclesiam Suam*, [#52] was also taken up by the Council in its teaching and ecumenical activity. Dialogue is not simply an exchange of ideas. In some way it is always an 'exchange of gifts' [#53].

There follows [# 29] a handbook of etiquette and diplomacy when engaging other Christians in dialogue. The Council's Decree on Ecumenism emphasizes the importance of 'every effort to eliminate words, judgments, and actions which do not respond to the condition of separated brethren with truth and fairness and so make mutual relations between them more difficult' [#54]. John Paul II recognises 'that The Decree approaches the question from the standpoint of the Catholic Church and refers to the criteria which she must apply in relation to other Christians'. However, he is protective of his own troops when sending them out in so docile and reconciliatory a fashion to face the opposition. He is quite clear that the other Christians should behave themselves in like manner. 'In all this, however, reciprocity is required. To follow these criteria is a commitment of each of the parties which desire to enter into dialogue and it is a precondition for starting such dialogue. It is necessary to pass from antagonism and conflict to a situation where each party recognizes the other as *partner*. When undertaking dialogue, *each side must presuppose in the other a desire for reconciliation, for unity in truth*. For this to happen, any display of mutual opposition must disappear. Only thus will dialogue help to overcome division and lead us closer to unity'. All of which is perfectly true and would be recognised as essential criteria and useful protocol for any conversation hoping to get anywhere. However, when the other side are sure that what you mean by 'a desire for reconciliation' and for 'unity in truth' is unconditional surrender to an already existing organisation, it becomes more difficult to make the removal of 'opposition' of any kind a prerequisite for negotiation.

Many might agree [# 30] that 'it can be said, with a sense of lively gratitude to the Spirit of Truth, that the Second Vatican Council was a blessed time, during which the bases for the Catholic Church's participation in ecumenical dialogue were laid'. However, to move from that to a later, much more restricted, elaboration of what that dialogue means, is not the same thing. In a section [#36] entitled 'Dialogue as a means of resolving disagreements', Catholic theologians engaged in ecumenical dialogue are reminded [quoting #61 of the Decree] that 'while standing fast by the teaching of the Church and searching together with separated brothers and sisters into the divine mysteries', they 'should act with love for truth, with charity, and with humility'. Again the ambiguity resides in the interpretation of the phrase 'standing fast by the teaching of the Church'. The paragraph which follows this one implies that such theologians should be ready to change much of what they brought to the table as preconceived theologies or ecclesiologies:

> Love for the truth is the deepest dimension of any authentic quest for full communion between Christians. Without this love it would be impossible to face the objective theological, cultural, psychological and social difficulties which appear when disagreements are examined. This dimension, which is interior and personal, must be inseparably accompanied by a spirit of charity and humility. There must be charity towards one's partner in dialogue, and humility with regard to the truth which comes to light and which might require a review of assertions and attitudes.

However, later commentary seems to take back with the left hand what the right has just conceded: 'With regard to the study of areas of disagreement, the Council requires that the whole body of doctrine be clearly presented'. It seems as if the elasticity of the Roman Catholic theologians is to be in the manner and the tone rather than in the content of what they bring to the dialogue. They are advised that 'the manner and method of expounding the Catholic faith should not be a hindrance to dialogue with our brothers and sisters [#62].' The Pope is certain that 'it is possible to profess one's faith and to explain its teaching in a way that is correct, fair and understandable, and which at the same time takes into account both the way of thinking and the actual historical experiences of the other party'. Such adjustment is in the area of diplomacy and presentation. It does not affect the 'truth', which is the legitimate inheritance, in his view, of the Roman Catholic tradition.

Full communion of course will have to come about through the acceptance of the whole truth into which the Holy Spirit guides Christ's disciples. Hence all forms of reductionism or facile 'agreement' must be avoided. Serious questions must be resolved, for if not, they will reappear at another time, either in the same terms or in a different guise.

John Paul II also points out [# 37] that the Decree *Unitatis Redintegratio* posits an order, or 'hierarchy', of truths, which vary in their relationship to the foundation of the Christian faith, and also [#38] 'a problem of the different formulations whereby doctrine is expressed in the various Churches and Ecclesial Communities'. We are urged to differentiate between fundamental and secondary formulations of truth. We are also required to examine the formulations of such truths in each of our Churches to establish whether or not they mean essentially the same thing:

> In the first place, with regard to doctrinal formulations which differ from those normally in use in the community to which one belongs, it is certainly right to determine whether the words involved say the same thing. This has been ascertained in the case for example of the recent common declarations signed by my Predecessors or by myself with the Patriarchs of Churches with which for centuries there have been disputes about Christology.

Again, this paragraph inspires the hope that ecumenical dialogue can achieve between our different Churches a formulation of the truths which we hold as fundamental in a language which we all find acceptable. But, again the text continues in a quotation which suggests that all such formulation has already been enunciated adequately by the Roman Catholic Church's Magisterium:

> As far as the formulation of revealed truths is concerned, the Declaration *Mysterium Ecclesiae* states: 'Even though the truths which the Church intends to teach through her dogmatic formulas are distinct from the changeable conceptions of a given epoch and can be expressed without them, nevertheless it can sometimes happen that these truths may be enunciated by the Sacred Magisterium in terms that bear traces of such conceptions. In view of this, it must be stated that the dogmatic *formulas* of the Church's Magisterium were from the very beginning suitable for communicating revealed truth, and that as they are they remain for ever suitable for communicating this truth to those who interpret them correctly' [#64].

Again the later commentary on this paragraph is ambiguous. The Pope is optimistic that 'ecumenical dialogue, which prompts the parties involved to question each other, to understand each other and to explain their positions to each other, makes surprising discoveries possible'. Whether these surprising discoveries are all on the side of the separated communities who suddenly realize that they really meant what Roman Catholics have been saying all along, or whether all parties involved, including Roman Catholics, discover from this dialogue other, more adequate, ways of formulating truths which we all recognize, is unclear. 'Intolerant polemics and controversies have made incompatible assertions out of what was really the result of two different ways of looking at the same reality' suggests the former. 'Nowadays we need to find the formula which, by capturing the reality in its entirety, will enable us to move beyond partial readings and eliminate false interpretations' leaves room for the latter. The advantage of Pope John Paul II's philosophising on the mystery of Christian unity is that it seems to leave open a certain number of interpretations. It appears to place the 'truth' of Christianity above and beyond any particular Church on earth and to invite all Christians to reach out, through ecumenical dialogue, towards that mysterious Truth.

> One of the advantages of ecumenism is that it helps Christian Communities to discover the unfathomable riches of the truth. Here too, everything that the Spirit brings about in 'others' can serve for the building up of all Communities [#65] and in a certain sense instruct them in the mystery of Christ. Authentic ecumenism is a gift at the service of truth.

So all are invited to participate in this edifying (in the original etymology of this word, which means 'to build up') exercise. And we do so not out of benevolence or compassion, but because we are all Christians and therefore committed to the work of God, which is Christian unity. 'It needs be reaffirmed in this regard that acknowledging our brotherhood is not the consequence of a large-hearted philanthropy or a vague family spirit. It is rooted in recognition of the oneness of Baptism and the subsequent duty to glorify God in his work'. Such mutual recognition, unthinkable a hundred years ago, is based upon an established and agreed acknowledgement of the ontological dimension of baptism, our being as Christians which cannot be gainsaid. 'This is something much more than an act of ecumenical courtesy; it constitutes a basic ecclesiological statement' in the words of Pope John Paul II.

Nor should the dialogue to which we are invited cause us to 'compromise ourselves or hide the genuine differences between us'. We come to the table in openness and honesty, leaving all our weapons and our armoury outside. We approach each other in humble deference to the mysterious Truth which we hold in common. At the last moment however we find that Roman Catholics have a litmus test for such Truth which is unavailable to other denominations:

> Finally, dialogue puts before the participants real and genuine disagreements in matters of faith. Above all, these disagreements should be faced in a sincere spirit of fraternal charity, of respect for the demands of one's own conscience and of the conscience of the other party, with profound humility and love for the truth. The examination of such disagreements has two essential points of reference: Sacred Scripture and the great Tradition of the Church. Catholics have the help of the Church's living Magisterium.

When eventually this encyclical puts before ecumenism the menu of disagreement, which has to be addressed before any 'unity' can be achieved, we detect what seems to be a hidden agenda unacceptable from the outset to other Christian denominations:

> It is already possible to identify the areas in need of fuller study before a true consensus of faith can be achieved: 1) the relationship between Sacred Scripture, as the highest authority in matters of faith, and Sacred Tradition, as indispensable to the interpretation of the Word of God; 2) the Eucharist, as the Sacrament of the Body and Blood of Christ, an offering of praise to the Father, the sacrificial memorial and Real Presence of Christ and the sanctifying outpouring of the Holy Spirit; 3) Ordination, as a Sacrament, to the threefold ministry of the episcopate, presbyterate and diaconate; 4) the Magisterium of the

Church, entrusted to the Pope and the Bishops in communion with him, understood as a responsibility and an authority exercised in the name of Christ for teaching and safeguarding the faith; 5) the Virgin Mary, as Mother of God and Icon of the Church, the spiritual Mother who intercedes for Christ's disciples and for all humanity [#79].

This comprehensive list of items which the separated Christians are expected to take on board before we even begin our dialogue, seems prohibitive. It reads as if Roman Catholics are imposing as pre-condition to any dialogue the three great white things which other denominations claim they have substituted for the true faith of Christianity: the Pope, the Host and the Virgin Mary. At its most negative level such a statement can be read as requiring from all participants before they attend discussions, a preliminary oath of allegiance to the doctrines of Papal Infallibility, Transubstantiation, and the Virgin Mary as Mediatrix of all Grace. This would be a hostile interpretation, but one which is justified from the language of the text. The difficulty throughout this encyclical is that its ambiguity allows for the most varied interpretation depending upon which sentence you read and which attitude you bring to the reading. Every positive and encouraging sentence seems to be undermined by the next one. So we have in the first half of one sentence a description of ecumenism as 'this courageous journey towards unity' immediately followed by a warning that 'transparency and the prudence of faith require us to avoid both false irenicism and indifference to the Church's ordinances'. Stop, go, stop, go, is the rhythm of each sentence and of the overall text. The next sentence again qualifies the previous warning with an upbeat exhortation: 'Conversely, that same transparency and prudence urge us to reject a halfhearted commitment to unity and, even more, a prejudicial opposition or a defeatism which tends to see everything in negative terms'.

And, again, having laid down the paralysing restrictions of total obedience to the Church's ordinances in every instance of such dialogue, we are told that 'to uphold a vision of unity which takes account of all the demands of revealed truth does not mean to put a brake on the ecumenical movement [#132]. On the contrary, it means preventing it from settling for apparent solutions which would lead to no firm and solid results' [#133].

Whatever about the ambiguity of the foregoing, #97 seems to leave very little room for manoeuvre when it comes to other denominations having to accept papal authority as this exists and is exercised in the Roman Catholic Church as at present:

> The Catholic Church, both in her *praxis* and in her solemn documents, holds that the communion of the particular Churches with the Church of Rome, and of their Bishops with the Bishop of Rome, is – in God's plan – an essential requisite of full and visible communion. Indeed full communion, of which the Eucharist is the highest sacramental manifestation, needs to be visibly expressed in a ministry in which all the Bishops recognize that they are united in Christ and all the faithful find confirmation for their faith. The first part of the Acts of the Apostles presents Peter as the one who speaks in the name of the apostolic group and who serves the unity of the community all the while respecting the authority of James, the head of the Church in Jerusalem. This function of Peter must continue in the Church so that under her sole Head, who is Jesus Christ, she may be visibly present in the world as the communion of all his disciples.

John Paul II is a philosopher as well as a theologian. His views on dialogue attempt to connect *'everything the Council defines as "dialogue"'* with what he refers to as 'today's *personalist way of thinking'*. Using this 'personalist philosophy' he understands 'the capacity for "dialogue"' as rooted in the nature of the person and the dignity of the person. He would claim that 'as seen by philosophy, this approach is linked to the Christian truth concerning man as expressed by the Council'. This is a very big claim and one which will be investigated in the following chapters of this book: how can any version of today's 'personalist philosophy' correspond with what the Second Vatican Council understands as 'dialogue' and presents in the context of a Christian anthropology?

Pope John Paul II was hopeful that the new millennium might bring with it a reunification of several of the separated Churches with Rome. No such reunification happened. Instead, in the very year of the millennium celebrations, two thousand years after the founding of Christianity, a 'declaration' was issued by the Congregation for the Doctrine of the Faith, 'on the unicity and salvific universality of Jesus Christ and the Church.' It was called *Dominus Jesus* after the two opening words of the text, as is Vatican wont. It was signed in Rome by Joseph Cardinal Ratzinger, Prefect of the Congregation for the Doctrine of the Faith, on the Feast of the Transfiguration of the Lord, 6 August 2000. It stated that 'the Sovereign Pontiff John Paul II, at the audience of 16 June 2000, granted to the undersigned Cardinal Prefect, with sure knowledge and by his apostolic authority, ratified and confirmed this Declaration, adopted in Plenary Session and ordered its publication'. It was released on 5 September 2000, two days after the controversial beatification of Pope Pius IX.

At a Vatican press conference on 5 September 2000 introducing the new statement, Cardinal Ratzinger was reported as saying that *Dominus Jesus* was a necessary response to 'the theology of religious pluralism', which is growing 'not only in theological circles, but also more generally in Catholic public opinion.' Many people today, he observed, view the Church's traditional claim to be the unique and universal means to salvation as 'a bit of fundamentalism which is an attack on the modern spirit and a menace to toleration and liberty.' Because of that attitude, many people see ecumenical dialogue as an end in itself: 'Dialogue – or rather the ideology of dialogue – becomes a substitute for missionary activity and for the urgency of an appeal to conversion.' This mistaken notion of dialogue, Cardinal Ratzinger said, emphasises not a search for objective and absolute truth, but a desire to put all religious beliefs on the same plane. And such dialogue gives rise to a 'false idea of tolerance,' which rejects the possibility of any objective truth.

Archbishop Tarcisio Bertone, Secretary of the Congregation for the Doctrine of the Faith, pointed out that *Dominus Jesus* does not contain any new teaching, but 'reaffirms and restates the doctrine of the Catholic faith' in answer to contemporary problems and theories. He emphasised that because it comes from the Holy See, with the explicit authorisation of the Pope, the document must be viewed as the teaching of the Magisterium, rather than just another theological opinion.

In ecumenical dialogue, then, it is never accurate to suggest that 'one religion is as good as another.' When the Church, as it engages in ecumenical dialogue, treats other partners with equal respect, this is out of recognition for 'the equal personal dignity of the parties in dialogue, not the doctrinal contents' of their beliefs.[5]

Archbishop Desmond Connell of Dublin who was also a member of the Congregation of the Doctrine of the Faith, was quoted as saying[6] that 'there are new things in this document' which were 'not to be found explicitly in texts of the Second Vatican Council'. The example he gave was the elucidation of the term 'subsists': the view that the one Church of Christ may subsist in various different Churches 'is rejected here'. And indeed there is a narrowing down of the polyvalent term used in the Vatican II Council to describe how 'the one and genuine Church of God is found in the Catholic Church and the certitude that it nonetheless extends beyond the Catholic Church' in the words of Cardinal Jan Willebrands, architect of the Council's Decree on Ecumenism.[7] *Dominus Jesus* makes this clarification with explicit reference in footnote 56 to a book by the liberation theologian Leonardo Boff, which had been previously condemned for such teachings: 'The interpretation of those who would derive from the formula *subsistit in* the thesis that the one Church of Christ could subsist also in non-Catholic Churches and ecclesial communities'. The declaration received in reply the following salvo from Boff himself:[8]

> With this document, as far as the Vatican hierarchy is concerned, Cardinal Ratzinger has dug the grave for ecumenism. The publication has the merit of clearing away any illusions about this. From now on, we know that we cannot count on the Vatican hierarchy in the search for spiritual and religious peace amongst humankind. On the contrary, with its capitalistic hoarding of divine truth, with its arrogant manner of dealing with others, Christianity in its Roman hierarchical form is actually a great obstacle to this search.

Dominus Jesus itself is a thirty-six page statement, divided into six chapters, and addressed to 'bishops, theologians, and all the Catholic faithful.' It has two main parts: the first focuses on the Church's relationship to non-Christian religions and the second addresses aspects of her relationship to Christians who are not members of the Roman Catholic Church.

The Church believes that in Jesus is found the one saving truth for the whole human race. The Church exists to proclaim this saving truth to every man, woman and child on the face of the earth. This truth claim about Jesus stands in direct contradiction to the prevailing philosophical and theological relativism of our time. Relativism, at its heart, is the denial of absolute truth. It states that no truth claims that apply to all people at all times can be made. The classic relativist expression today is, 'you have your truth and I have mine.' All truths are equally valid in this scheme of things. To make a truth claim is considered bad form, the height of arrogance, and an imposition on another's individual liberty.

Dominus Jesus points out that this culture of relativism has undermined the clarity and conviction of some theologians and teachers about the Church's unique mission. For example, some have come to believe that evangelization, the Church's very reason for being, is an expression of cultural imperialism and a violation of religious liberty. They state that since all truth is relative, no religion can claim to have the truth. All religions are said to possess some measure of the truth about God and therefore are equally valid roads to him. The Church can no longer claim that Jesus is *the* only Saviour of the world, but only that he is *a* saviour of the world. To make an exclusive claim about the uniqueness of Jesus is to impose one's own beliefs on another.

The logic of this argument has led to a steady erosion of the Church's missionary zeal. If all the religions of the world provide equally valid roads to God, why should the Catholic Church seek to convert anyone? Wouldn't it be better simply to help someone become a better Buddhist, Moslem, or Hare Krishna? Some have gone so far as to raise the question whether missionary work, in the traditional sense of 'making disciples of all nations,' is still relevant. Instead, they propose the promotion of human development as a viable alternative. Thus, the Church's mission is narrowed to works of social solidarity instead of the proclamation of the Gospel. The mission is limited to earthly goals like relieving poverty, and fighting political injustices. The larger eternal realities such as relieving ultimate despair through the hope of eternal life in Jesus are abandoned.

The goal of *Dominus Jesus* is to clear up the confusion caused by this kind of thinking and to inspire the faithful to take up the

Church's mission to the nations with renewed conviction. Those who drafted the document want to restore the Church's resolve and to inflame her passion to fulfill Jesus' command to 'make disciples of all nations.'

Much of the confusion about her mission has surfaced within the context of inter-religious dialogue, that is, the Church's attempt to build relationships of mutual respect and understanding with non-Christian religions. Some who have participated in the dialogue have proposed that the Church no longer consider other religions the subject of her missionary efforts, but instead replace the goal of conversion with meaningful dialogue. Since every religious tradition has its own way to God and means of salvation, conversion is no longer necessary.

Dominus Jesus makes it clear that inter-religious dialogue 'certainly does not replace, but rather accompanies the mission *ad gentes*' (to the nations). In fact, properly understood, inter-religious dialogue should be seen as 'part of the Church's evangelizing mission.' (DJ#2) The Catholic Church 'rejects nothing of what is true and holy in these religions.' (DJ#2) Indeed, she even acknowledges the possibility of salvation for 'those who, through no fault of their own, do not know the Gospel of Christ or his Church, but who nevertheless seek God with a sincere heart, and moved by grace, try in their actions to do his will as they know it through the dictates of their conscience.' (*Lumen Gentium* #16)

Those who wish to reduce the Church's mandate from evangelization to dialogue often point to the passage from *Lumen Gentium* as support for their position. They conclude that the Church herself is claiming that all that is needed for salvation is 'a sincere heart' or 'an upright heart' so there is no need for an explicit proclamation of the gospel.

The Church however, draws the exact opposite conclusion in the same paragraph. Finally, *Dominus Jesus* makes the point that even those who are saved without explicit knowledge of

Jesus are saved because of him: 'all men and women who are saved share, though differently, in the same mystery of salvation in Jesus Christ through his Spirit.' (DJ#2)

Jesus is 'the mediator and the fullness of all revelation,' and 'in this definitive Word of his revelation, God has made himself known in the fullest possible way. He has revealed to mankind who he is.' (DJ#5) All that God desires to reveal about himself to the human race has been perfectly revealed in Jesus. *Dominus Jesus* makes clear that 'there is only one salvific economy of the One and Triune God.' (DJ#12) That is, there is no other plan of salvation; there are no other saviours, no separate mission of the Holy Spirit or the Logos or any other means by which men can be saved. In the fourth and fifth Chapters, *Dominus Jesus* notes that the salvation promised by Jesus Christ comes through the Catholic Church, his 'bride' and Mystical Body. The Catholic Church – defined as the Church that has maintained apostolic succession – is the one true Church.

While the document acknowledges that some Orthodox Churches, which have maintained apostolic succession although they do not accept the primacy of Peter, represent the true Church, other Christian bodies do not enjoy the same status. Through baptism, it says, the members of these Christian ecclesial bodies are 'incorporated in Christ' and maintain 'a certain communion, albeit imperfect,' with the Church.[9]

This document caused negative reactions from many non-Catholics throughout the world. That 'Ecclesial communities that have not preserved the valid episcopate and the genuine and integral substance of the Eucharistic mystery are not Churches in the proper sense', drew a critical response from the Anglican Archbishop of Canterbury, Dr George Carey. This statement, he said, fails to represent 'the deeper understanding that has been achieved through ecumenical dialogue and co-operation during the past thirty years.' He added that the Anglican Church 'believes itself to be part of the one, holy, catholic, and apostolic Church of Christ.' Martin Marty, an American Protestant commentator, suggested that the CDF is asserting about the Roman Catholic Church: 'We are the oldest ... we are the best ... we are the only Church.'[10]

The Declaration *Dominus Jesus* both in its content and its timing forces Roman Catholics to reassess their situation and define exactly what they mean by 'dialogue' in the twenty-first century. If Roman Catholics are bound by the terms of this recent declaration, then the only kind of dialogue permitted to them would seem to be 'educational dialogue' as this will be described in Chapter Three, because as John Garvey, Orthodox Archbishop of New York, sums up his reading of *Dominus Jesus*: 'The Catholic Church has nothing to learn and everything to teach'.[11]

Having decided what dialogue could mean for Roman Catholics it would then be important to advertise this as the only form available or permitted, otherwise they could be guilty of corporate injustice wherever they seek to engage others in this exercise:[12]

> The Declaration has other defects. One of them is the idea that dialogue with the world religions is compatible with the intention of making converts. Dialogue is a conversation based on trust and mutual acceptance, in which the partners feel free to reveal their own problems and unresolved questions. Dialogue is an unguarded conversation. Dialogue is an exchange that transforms both partners, leading them to a better self-understanding, revealing to them the prejudice mediated by their own tradition, and making them aspire to a more authentic and enlarged possession of their own religion. It would be utterly deceitful to lure a partner into dialogue, attempt to create a community of trust in which the partner is willing to expose the weakness of his own tradition, and then abuse this confidence in an

effort to persuade the partner to change his or her religion. It may happen, of course, that in such a trusting dialogue a partner decides to move to another religious tradition. But interreligious dialogue would be a form of manipulation if its aim were to make Christians of the participants. The proposal that dialogue and convert-making can go together is unethical.

This is Gregory Baum reacting to the analysis of dialogue with other religions. On the question of the timing of the Declaration in the year of the Millennium of Christianity and immediately after the controversial canonisation of Pius IX, the same Orthodox Archbishop of New York already quoted had this to say:

No pope ever did more to cement a wedge into place between Catholicism and Orthodoxy than Pius IX, not to speak of the distance he put between Rome and every other Christian communion. Although Orthodoxy could not accept Roman claims to jurisdiction over all Churches, it could accept the Bishop of Rome as first among equal patriarchs, if he were willing to abandon the notion of universal jurisdiction. When Pius IX introduced the definition of the pope as infallible in matters of faith and morals when he speaks *ex cathedra* – when, that is, Vatican I made the pope a bishop uniquely unlike all other bishops – there was, Orthodox thinkers would argue, a move towards heresy on Rome's part.[13]

The 'declaration' elicited criticism from Roman Catholic prelates also. Cardinal Roger Mahony, Archbishop of Los Angeles said that 'The tone of *Dominus Jesus* may not fully reflect the deeper understanding that has been achieved through ecumenical and interreligious dialogues over these last thirty years or more.'[14] Rembert Weakland, Archbishop of

Milwaukee, suggested: 'Unfortunately, *Dominus Jesus* does not take into account the enormous progress made after Vatican II in the mutual recognition of each other's baptisms and the ecclesial significance of such recognition. What is disappointing about this document is that so many of our partners will find its tone heavy, almost arrogant and condescending. To them it is bound to seem out of keeping with the elevated and open tone of the documents of Vatican II. It ignores all of the ecumenical dialogues of these last thirty-five years, as if they did not exist. None of the agreed statements are cited.'[15]

Battlelines have been drawn for and against this document. The progressives would hold that Marco Politi seems to have got it right. In an essay in the 6 September 2000 issue of *La Repubblica,* an Italian newspaper, Politi wrote that everything flowing out of the Vatican this summer is connected. The connection between the Vatican's scathing response to World Pride, the document on divorce and remarriage, the note on sister Churches, the beatification of Pius IX, and now *Dominus Jesus*, is the looming conclave. Ratzinger and those like him in the curia are doing everything possible to close doors and windows in an effort to make it difficult for John Paul II's successor to reverse their policies. Politi ends his essay by asking where the Pope stands, and his punchline is powerful: The battle, he says, also runs though Wojtyla's soul.

Readers will readily recall, he says, the image of a solitary John Paul II at the Western Wall in Jerusalem last March, deep in prayer, leaving behind a handwritten note apologizing to Jews for the failings of the Church. Recall, too, the invitation he sent to leaders of other world religions to meet for prayer at Assisi. The Pope asked no one to convert, insisted that no one accept Jesus – instead he reached out in humility, using the common language of penance and prayer. And in so doing, he dazzled the world.

How do we reconcile that behaviour with what is in *Dominus Jesus*?

The fact is that Catholics have a serious gap between our practice of dialogue, as illustrated by the Pope himself in his encounters with members of other religions, and the official theology of the Church. It is one of the paradoxes of a papacy riddled with contradictions.

We have, however, been given two paths – a profound show of respect and regard for other religions or a bullying document that demeans the beliefs of others. For those of us who are happy to live day-to-day in increasingly pluralistic circumstances, the choice is simple. Join, if only figuratively, in the prayer at the Western Wall. Stand in awe of the response our Islamic brothers and sisters make to the call to prayer. Rejoice that the Protestant Churches across the street, our sister Churches indeed, are no longer perceived as sinister and suspect.

And all the while, hold deeply the truths of our Catholic Christianity, expressed in that great creed.[16]

On the other hand, the Bulletin of the Society of S Pius X, March 2003 No. 51, holds that this declaration is as heretical as Vatican II was because it does not condemn all heretics and preach that there can be no salvation outside the Roman Catholic Church:

> Vatican II's error has remained in the *DJ*. It continues to teach that the heretical and schismatic communities would be part of the 'Church of Christ,' although enjoying supposed means of salvation presenting 'deficiencies,' and thus less full, and for this reason finding themselves in a position of inferiority in relation to the Catholic Church. But this inferiority would be without influence on what concerns obtaining salvation, and so totally theoretical. All this is absurd and incoherent, and represents the negation of the truth of divine and Catholic Faith according to which only the Catholic Church is the one true Church of Christ,

immutable and faithful through the centuries, outside of which there is no salvation.

Notes

1 His Holiness Pope John Paul II, *Ut Unum Sint*, 'That They May Be One', May 25, 1995.

2 SECOND VATICAN ECUMENICAL COUNCIL, Declaration on Religious Freedom, *Dignitatis Humanae*, 1.

3 Cf. Apostolic Letter, *Tertio Millennio Adveniente* (10 November 1994), 16: *AAS* 87 (1995), 15.

4 10: Cf. SECOND VATICAN ECUMENICAL COUNCIL, Dogmatic Constitution on the Church, *Lumen Gentium*, 14.

5 Quotations in the last 3 paragraphs taken from *AD2000*, Vol. 13 No. 9 (October 2000), p. 3.

6 *Irish Times*, October 12, 2000. For much of this commentary on *Dominus Jesus* I am indebted to my confrere Fintan Lyons OSB and his article: 'Where is the Church?' *Doctrine and Life*, January 2001, pp. 8-17.

7 Gérard Philips, 'Dogmatic Constitution on the Church. History of the Constitution', in H. Vorgrimler, *Commentary on the Documents of Vatican II*, Vol. I (London, Burns & Oates, 1967), p. 108.

8 *Le réseau Culture et Foi* – 2000-2001 – Translation by Michael Seifert.

9 What I have used here as a sympathetic summary of this declaration has been taken in reduced form from *Dominus Jesus* by Peter Herbeck www.renewalministries.net.

10 In 'Rome and Relativism: *Dominus Jesus* & the CDF', *Commonweal* Oct 20, 2000.

11 John Garvey, Orthodox parish priest in New York, an original article in *Commonweal* reprinted and expanded in *Doctrine and Life*, January, 2001, p. 19.

12 Gregory Baum: *The Ecumenist*, vol. 37, no. 4, Fall 2000.

13 John Garvey, Orthodox parish priest in New York, an original article in *Commonweal* reprinted and expanded in *Doctrine and Life*, January, 2001, p. 19.

14 Cited in Peter Chirico, '*Dominus Jesus* as an Event', *America* (March 26, 2001), pp. 24-28 (27).

15 Ibid.

16 As reported in *National Catholic Reporter*, September 15, 2000.

CHAPTER III

DIALOGUE IN THE WORKS
OF MARTIN BUBER

Dialogue for Buber could not really be described as either an activity or an attitude, it is more fundamentally a way of being. As such, it cannot be ascribed to an institution except insofar as this corporate body might legislate for, or foster the growth of this reality in its members. As a way of being it would set itself up against the traditional way of being of our Western European Culture, which, according to Buber, would militate against the realization of genuine dialogue within our civilization, preferring as it does, to emphasize the autonomous self-contained growth of the individual rather than the other-orientated development of the human person.

Buber would place the locus of truth, not in the subject (as in 'subjective truth') or in the object (as in 'objective truth'), but in the category of 'the between'. Whatever the truth may mean in other areas, in the sphere of the interhuman it means that people communicate themselves to each other as they are. In such a view, the counterpart to the 'subject', in terms of my becoming a person, is not an 'object' but an 'other'. The other is what generates personhood. I am born a man or a woman, an individual, but I *become* a person by spilling out into the space between myself and the other. This movement of 'exodus' from my self-contained reality, which is inspired by the 'other', constitutes the specific dimension of 'personality'.

The distinction between humanity and the animal kingdom is a qualitative gap which Buber calls 'distance'. Humans alone of all creatures are capable of distancing themselves from all that is not this self. This capacity makes us 'individual' and makes of nature 'a world'. Only humans can have a world. The animal is like 'a fruit in its skin', the reality around it can never become detached enough to be, or to be recognized for, what it is in itself.

Having established this primal distance which activates our individuation and gives birth to each 'subjectivity' and which constitutes humanity, distinguishing it from the animal kingdom, Buber goes on to show that a difference almost as radical distinguishes the 'individual' from the 'person'. We are born individuals, but we become persons: the first is a necessity, the second a possibility. The 'distance' which breaks our natural union with the environment, is the necessary preliminary to all relationship. It is the being of humanness and, as such, separates us from total identification with nature and all other living creatures.

The unusual fact about humanity, which Buber claims to point to, is that this reality of our being 'separated' is not enough to express the full possibility of our being. In order to find meaning, to become fully ourselves, we need others. Buber expresses this in the aphorism 'all real living is meeting'. The dimension of 'personhood', as opposed to mere humanity, is achieved, not by securing the identity which we have been born into, in the face of the animal kingdom, but by sacrificing this autonomy in favour of communion with others.

Technically speaking, we could use the work 'ontological' to describe the 'primal distance' which separates us from the animal kingdom and thus establishes the important realm of the 'between' which provides us with the locus of truth and the seedbed of personhood. The word 'ontological' tries to state the fact that such essential distance is not one which is actively established by ourselves at a psychological level, it is a necessary event which takes place at the level of our being without the co-operation of our psychological awareness. It concerns the essential being of our humanity. It is not a matter of choice or freedom. It is the way we are. It constitutes our being as men and women. This is what we mean when we describe the primacy of 'distance' and the category of the 'between' as 'ontological'. 'Distance provides the human situation; relation provides our becoming in that situation'.[1]

Distancing achieves a hardening of the quicksands of nature. It constructs a platform upon which the history of humankind and of the world can begin. It provides a stage on which the drama of human existence becomes a possibility. It does not cause this possibility to happen, it merely provides its essential basis. It insulates an area cordoned off from the all-pervading law of nature. This area then becomes the only space in nature where the full reality of humanity can be achieved.

The real question is what we do with the possibility opened for us by this primal setting at a distance. This fact of distance between humankind and the world makes it possible to re-establish contact with the world and this contact involves a choice: the distance can be solidified into a wall or it can be spanned by a bridge. In either case a type of relationship will be established with the world which will determine both the kind of world we choose to meet and the kind of human being we choose to become. In fact, there are not two distinct kinds of 'world', nor are there two types of people, but the quality of relationship allows us to say that the one who decides to solidify the primal distance into a wall is a different kind to those who turn this gap into a space of meeting between themselves and all that steps up to meet them.

The first kind of human being, in Buber's terminology, is an individual; the second is a person. The first leads a life of monologue; the second a life of dialogue. For the first, the world which it confronts is an object, allowing itself to be manipulated; for the second the world is a presence, which defies the opposition between subject and object. The first kind of contact is called by Buber an 'I-It' relationship, the second he calls an 'I-Thou' relationship.

It is not possible to break up these terms into units of 'I', 'It' and 'Thou'. Each term is a complex unity which defines the totality of the relationship as well as the constituent elements which comprise it. The world of 'It' stands opposite in indifference as an object, because the relationship of the 'I' determines this mode of being for both. The world of 'Thou' awaits the I's response as a presence, which is called forth by the openness in the relationship of the 'I'. The first 'I' is an individual; the second is a person. Buber classifies the first as one who lives by appearances and the second as one who lives from the essence. The being (*esse*) of the first is situated within itself; the being (*esse*) of the second is situated in the space between (*inter*) the self and the world, it is our interest (*interesse*) in others.

It is not as if one of these relationships were 'wrong' and the other 'right'. Both are necessary for human existence. The real question is how to combine them successfully, without letting the second be annihilated by the first, for such would be the 'natural' inclination of the 'I-It' relationship.

This 'I-It' relationship refuses to allow anyone or anything that steps up to meet us have any significant existence of their own. Everything has to be arranged according to the law and order of the individual's mind. The world is no more than an extension of the 'I'. Relationship with it is domination, exploitation, manipulation. Whether it meets people, things, environment or natural resources, its instinct is to harness these to its own vision or purpose. The 'I' has a preconceived understanding and plan about the way things or people are, or the way they ought to be. Everything and everyone we meet are expected to conform to these norms. At the level of politics this becomes totalitarian or imperial colonization; at the level of education it means propaganda; its ethics are doctrinaire and its art strictly formal. Buber himself describes the 'I-It' relationship as follows:[2]

> I-It is the primary word of experiencing and using. It takes place within a man and not between him and the world. Hence it is entirely subjective and lacking in mutuality. Whether in knowing, feeling, or acting, it is the typical subject-object relationship. It is always mediate and indirect, dealing with objects in terms of categories and connections, and hence is comprehensible and orderable. It is significant only in connection and not in itself. The It and I-It may equally well be a he, a she, an animal, a thing, a spirit, or even a God, without a change in the primary word … Man can live continuously and securely in the world of It, but if he lives only in this world he is not a man.

This relationship, and the 'I-It' connection in the works of Buber are not to be identified with evil. Both the 'I-It' and the 'I-Thou' relationship are necessary for human existence. The first, in its reliability and ordered world, sustains humankind. Although one cannot meet others in it, it is only through this dimension that one can make oneself understood by others. The 'I-Thou' relationship is not, on the other hand, an unqualified good. In its lack of measure, continuity and order it could be destructive of life. Buber's advice to humankind is not to abandon the work of constructing an ordered world in favour of total surrender to the search for an 'I-Thou' relationship. His advice would be to carry on this work, but not to neglect the call to this second dimension, without which work of any other kind is meaningless. If we neglect to stand also in mutual relationship with the world, we can be as successful as we like in the construction of ourselves and of a world, but we shall not reach the dimension of personhood:[3]

Each of us is encased in an armour whose task is to ward off signs. Signs happen to us without respite, living means being addressed, we would only have to present ourselves and to perceive. But the risk is too dangerous for us, the soundless thunderings seem to threaten us with annihilation, and from generation to generation we perfect the defense apparatus ... Each of us is encased in an armour which we soon, out of familiarity, no longer notice ... The interlocking sterilized system into which all this only needs to be dovetailed is man's titanic work.

European civilization has been, for the most part, such a titanic work. The guardians of this civilization will hold that we cannot allow ourselves to pursue such useless and destructive impulses as those that lead us towards the 'I-Thou' relationship. Such would inevitably mean the destruction of our ordered society and the removal of all the benefits which our civilization has won. Buber is aware of this criticism and these fears:[4]

So now the *adversarius* sits, facing me in his actual form as he appears in accordance with the spirit of the time, and speaks, more above and beyond me than towards and to me, in accents and attitude customary in the universal duel, free of personal relation.

'In all this the actuality of our present life, the conditioned nature of life as a whole, is not taken into account. All that you speak of takes place in the never-never-land, not in the social context of the world in which we spend our days, and by which if by anything our reality is defined. Your "two men" sit on a solitary seat, obviously during a holiday journey. In a big city office you would not be able to let them sit, they would not reach the "sacramental" there ... That may be quite interesting for people who are not taken up with any duty. But is the business employee to "communicate himself without reserve" to his colleagues? Is the worker at the conveyor belt to "feel himself addressed in what he experiences"? In spite of all reference to concreteness, all this is pre-war individualism in a revised edition.'

And I, out of a deep consciousness of how almost impossible it is to think in common, if only in opposition, where there is no common experience, reply ... 'There is no ordering of dialogue. It is not that you *are* to answer but that you *are able*. You are really able. The life of dialogue is no privilege of intellectual activity like dialectic. It does not begin in the upper story of humanity. It begins no higher than where humanity begins. There are no gifted and ungifted here, only those who withhold themselves.'

There is a truth, a way of being, a way of living in the world, Buber holds, which is the truth of individuality; it is a monologue, a self-constructed world. But it is human truth and not the truth about humanity. This truth is to be found in the life of dialogue:[5]

> It is a matter of renouncing the pantechnical mania or habit with its easy 'mastery' of every situation; of taking everything up into the might of dialogue of the genuine life ... The task becomes more and more difficult, and more and more essential, the fulfilment more and more impeded and more and more rich in decision. All the regulated chaos of the age waits for the break-through, and wherever a man perceives and responds, he is working to that end.

Buber is not suggesting that we replace the 'I-It' relationship with the 'I-Thou'. He is promoting the cause of mutually enriching harmony between these two relationships, which would allow the second to provide the first with meaning. He calls for 'an order of work in which business is so continually soaked in vital dialogic as the tasks to be fulfilled by it allow'.[6]

However, it is not enough simply to describe or to applaud this 'dialogical principle'. We must try to articulate the grammar of this second relationship, to explain what is meant by dialogue, and to show how it is possible to achieve a life-giving harmony between the 'I-It' and the 'I-Thou'.

We have seen how the primary setting at a distance provides the situation which allows for the possibility of a two-fold relationship with the world. The primary words 'I-It' and 'I-Thou' express two possible relationships issuing from this situation. The first of these is a centripetal movement towards the centre of the self, a walling off of the world, a concentration on the 'inner life' as source of all truth and meaning. The second movement is a centrifugal one, which goes out to meet the world in an instinct of communion. It situates the source of truth and meaning beyond the periphery of the self, in the realm of 'the between'. Here the self is completely open to whatever presence addresses it:[7]

> I term basic movement an essential action of man (it may be understood as an 'inner' action, but it is not there unless it is there to the very tension of the eye's muscles and the very action of the foot as it walks), round which an essential attitude is built up ... The basic movement in the life of dialogue is the turning towards the other. That, indeed, seems to happen every hour and quite trivially. If you look at someone and address him you turn to him, of course with the body, but also in the requisite measure with the soul, in that you direct your attention to him. But what of all this is an essential action, done with the essential being? In this way, that

out of the incomprehensibility of what lies to hand this one person steps forth and becomes a presence.

Dialogical life is not produced by this movement. The movement is one of its elements. It prepares us for it. Dialogue itself cannot be reduced to any reality within one person. It is not physical or psychological although it catches these up into itself. It is an ontological movement which *can* carry the self on the surge of the wave of meeting, by assuming the dialogical attitude.

> The *Thou* meets me through grace – it is not found by seeking. But by my speaking of the primary word to it, it is an act of my being, is indeed *the* act of my being.
>
> The *Thou* meets me. But I step into direct relation with it. Hence the relation means being chosen and choosing, suffering and action in one; just as any action of the whole being, which means the suspension of all partial actions and consequently of all sensations of actions grounded only in their particular limitation, is bound to resemble suffering.
>
> The primary word *I-Thou* can be spoken only with the whole being. Concentration and fusion into the whole being can never take place through my agency, nor can it ever take place without me. I become through my relation to the *Thou*; as I become I, I say *Thou*. All real living is meeting.

This quotation from Buber's most famous book *I and Thou*[8] sums up the relationship of dialogue. Unlike the life of the individual, the life of monologue, the life of dialogue does not find its source or its agency within the self. It is not a centripetal movement to and from the self as source, an odyssey which wanders through the world and brings back all into the precincts of the self. It is a centrifugal movement of exodus which spills my being over into the world in the trust and expectation that in this space outside myself, the 'between', I shall become fully 'I' by contacting the 'other' as 'Thou'. The relationship is direct. Unlike the movement of monologue where I strengthen the distance which makes up the between, the movement of dialogue dissolves everything that comes between the I and the other. It suppresses the 'distance' which encircles my identity and provides an immediate contact with the 'other'. I may not automatically meet the Thou; the potential Thou may withhold this response; I may be left in the unanswered openness of my primal movement. None of these possibilities belie the fundamental reality which exists in potency in each one of us, and whose activation constitutes the mainspring of human life. The 'I-Thou' relationship is *the* possibility open to us as human beings. The life of dialogue must, therefore, be pursued as part of our birthright, for only through it can we reach authentic human existence. However, this birthright cannot be simply inherited, it has to be earned.

The Different forms of the 'I-Thou' relationship of Dialogue
The difficulties involved in adequately conceptualizing the 'I-Thou' relationship must not persuade us to withdraw from the task. It is possible to establish certain constant factors which, if they do not define the reality in question, at least stake out the conditions which make such a relationship possible, and without which it cannot exist in any form whatever.

This relationship, which makes us present to 'the other' in an immediate and total way, is not just an exquisite moment of human existence, it is necessary for full accomplishment of this existence. Without it, Buber would claim, we are not fully human. He does not suggest that this is the only kind of relationship possible, nor would he claim that it is possible to realize it in any situation at any given time. What he does say is that unless this threshold has been reached at some time or other during the life of each one of us, we do not accede to the dimension of personhood. The 'I-Thou' relationship is the one ingredient essential to human existence as a person. Without it we can survive, but survival is hardly worthwhile. We survive as individuals, but we live as persons. Never to accede to this dimension of personhood means never to have really lived. It is also necessary to explain that we are constitutionally incapable of full-time commitment to such relationship. The fact that it is essential to the full realization of our humanity does not make it identifiable with the humanity to which it gives birth. It is essential to, but not exhaustive of, all genuine human being.

The task of 'explaining' this relationship is, by nature, an attempt to transfer the 'I-Thou' into the ordered world of 'I-It'. Such an attempt is necessarily a conceptual and logicizing task and one which is necessary if we are to discuss this reality in the ordinary terms of human discourse. However, such a necessity of using the weak and indispensable tools of human logic should not blind us to the essentially inexpressible nature of the reality itself. With such cautionary warnings as a necessary introduction, it is still possible to clarify somewhat the reality which Buber points to when he insists that 'dialogue' is the *sine qua non* of all personal existence.

Perhaps the easiest way to begin is with a diagram showing the full spectrum of possible relationships between the 'I' and the world.

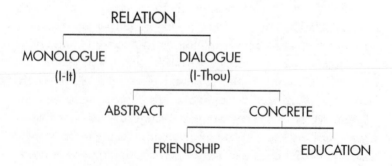

In this diagram I have reduced the total spectrum of possible relationship to the sphere of the inter-human. For Buber, there are also the relationships we have with nature, with what he calls the *geistige Wesenheiten* (a difficult term to translate, referring to 'things of the spirit' or 'spiritual beings' including works of art) and with God. Since these do not enter the present discussion, it is preferable to ignore them and concentrate upon the specifically inter-human dimension.

In all the above we are involved with the category of 'relation'. It is not as though 'I-Thou' were 'relation' and 'I-It' some form of 'non-relation'. Both these primary words are kinds of relationship with the world of other human beings. This should make it clear that it is always possible to substitute an 'I-It' relationship for all three forms of the 'I-Thou' relation shown in the diagram: the abstract, the concrete, and within this latter form, the two modalities of friendship and education.

In the first part of this chapter we have seen the difference between the 'I-It' and the 'I-Thou' as basic attitudes towards the 'other'. Here, in this section, the task is to elucidate the differences between the three forms of dialogue listed under the heading of 'I-Thou' relationship with other people.

What all these forms of dialogue have in common is more important than what distinguishes them. This common factor is what Buber calls 'inclusion' (*Umfassung*). It is by this term that he identifies the reality of dialogue:[9]

> A relation between persons that is characterized in more or less degree by the element of inclusion may be termed a dialogical relation.

The three elements of 'inclusion' are: first, a relation of no matter what kind between two persons; second, an event experienced by them in common, in which at least one of them actively participates; third, the fact that 'this one person, without forfeiting anything of the felt reality of his activity, at the same time lives through the common event from the standpoint of the other'.[10]

The first element requires that 'each of the participants really has in mind the other or others in their present and particular being and turns to them with the intention of establishing a living mutual relation between himself and them'. The presupposition of all dialogue is that at least one of the partners be a person as opposed to an individual. The dialogue of 'friendship' involves two partners who are fully persons and who turn to each other in a mutuality which is fully equal and reciprocated. This is probably the highest form of dialogue and the one that is easiest to understand.

Education is a lesser form of this dialogue by which this reality of being is transmitted from one full person to another potential person. Here the mutuality, although present, is not symmetrical. The educating partner has to make up the deficiency of response from the side of the unformed partner, and lead this latter to the full equality and mutuality of fully developed personality. Neither friendship nor education are possible when neither partner is a person, when the relation between them is one of projected monologue. 'I know people', Buber says, 'who are absorbed in social activity and yet have never spoken from being to being with a fellow man'. And he goes on to say that 'being, lived in monologue, will not, even in the tenderest intimacy, grope out over the outlines of the self'.[11]

What both these modalities of dialogue, that of friendship and that of education, require as a basis is 'trust'. There can be no dialogue at all, and no education or friendship, if this element is not established in the first place. However, when this 'acceptance' or 'trust' has been established, this is only the beginning of the relationship. The second element is 'an event experienced by them in common'. And here we must distinguish between the reality of 'acceptance' and another important term in Buber's description of dialogue, the equally important notion of 'confirmation'. In both education and friendship, this second element of the dialogue is essential:[12]

> The basis of man's life with man is twofold, and it is one – the wish of every man to be confirmed as what he is, even as what he can become, by men; and the innate capacity in man to confirm his fellow men in this way. That this capacity lies so immeasurably fallow constitutes the real weakness and questionableness of the human race: actual humanity exists only where this capacity unfolds.

Acceptance is not enough to establish the genuine life of dialogue. In education, especially, this other dimension of trust which will involve confirmation 'of what a man can become' may, indeed, involve the rejection of what someone actually is, so that the reality of what he may become has room to emerge:[13]

> Conflicts also have an educational value, so long as they occur in a healthy atmosphere of mutual confidence.
> 'A conflict with a pupil is the supreme test for the educator', (Buber) asserted. But the teacher must use insight during this battle for the truth. If he wins the conflict, he has to help the vanquished to endure defeat; and if he cannot overcome the pupil's will, then he must find the word of love which will make the conflict part of the educational process.

This confirmation, sometimes even in conflict, is true also for friendship. It is not just enough to accept the other as he or she actually is. It is also important to assert the truth of the real being of both partners, to confirm it. This aspect of Buber's dialogue has been too much neglected. It corresponds to the ideas of several other philosophers who have written about friendship, from Aristotle to Neitzsche. True confirmation means that one confirms one's partner as this existing being even while one opposes him/her. It is at base a trust that the truth will not destroy, but will rather confirm, the becoming-human of the other. It is a confirmation of being as opposed to appearing.

In an essay on friendship, Emerson expresses a similar thought: 'I hate', he says, 'where I looked for a manly furtherance, or at least a manly resistance, to find a mush of concession. Better be a nettle in the side of your friend than his echo.' And Neitzsche in that section of *Thus Spoke Zarathustra* which speaks of 'the friend' says: 'If you want a friend, you must be willing to wage war for him: and to wage war, you must be *capable* of being an enemy. You should honour even the enemy in your friend. Can you go near to your friend without going over to him? In your friend you should possess your best enemy … Are you pure air and solitude and bread and medicine to your friend?'

This is what Buber means when he distinguishes between acceptance and 'confirmation' in both friendship and education. Confirmation implies the rejection of seeming in favour of being. We confirm the being of the other when, and as, we meet it in his presence. The full mutuality of being to being is experienced in friendship. Here confirmation becomes fully inclusive. Once we leave the sphere of monologue, once the self pours out into the realm of the between, which alone creates the form of dialogue, it becomes necessary to find some guarantee of the being which we extend into this common realm. It is not possible for us to provide for ourselves the stamp of authenticity for this being of personhood. The confirmation must come from another.

In all forms of dialogue there must be real presence of the partners. The difference between the educational form and the form of friendship is that the movement from the teacher to the pupil is stronger and more creative than that which comes from the pupil to the teacher. The relation is not symmetrical. This does not happen because of some faulty exercise of the presence of either partner. It stems from the reality of the situation in which 'mature being' faces 'being in the process of becoming'. But there must be mutuality in this as in any dialogical relationship:[14]

> But this mutuality – that is what constitutes the peculiar nature of the relation in education – cannot be one of inclusion, although the true relation of the educator to the pupil is based on inclusion. No other relation draws its inner life like this one from the element of inclusion, but no other is in that regard like this, completely directed to one-sidedness, so that if it loses one-sidedness, it loses essence.

The peculiarity of the educational form of dialogue is that the educator is required to exercise the full reality of the 'I-Thou' relationship in face of a special brand of other, one which is there and yet is not fully there. We have to set up a relationship of mutuality with the real presence of the child as the child actually is, but we must not allow this to confirm the child, to restrict the child to this mode of being. The child must always be opening up to the further possibilities which are within the child's reach. Growth prevents the possibility of stopping at any particular point on the way. The full flowering of mutuality would be the confirmation of the completion of both partners. It is therefore not possible until the child is fully there, and wherever it is attempted, during the time of education, it is destructive of the educational relation.

> But however intense the mutuality of giving and taking with which he is bound to his pupil, inclusion cannot be mutual in this case. He experiences the pupil's being educated, but the pupil cannot experience the educating

of the educator. The educator stands at both ends of the common situation, the pupil only at one end. In the moment when the pupil is able to throw himself across and experience from over there, the educative relation would be burst asunder, or change into friendship.

This quotation[15] summarizes the distinction which must be made between the dialogue of education and the dialogue of friendship. Unlike the situation of friendship, where mutuality, inclusion and the responsibility for the relation are equally shared, in education the responsibility for the total situation lies with the teacher. The pupil is responsible only for his own presence. He or she has none for the relationship itself. The teacher is required to monitor the relationship from both sides. This means that certain characteristics and capacities are demanded of him or her and, without these, he or she has no being as a teacher.

As teachers, we must, first of all, have the capacity to recognize the 'reality' of the particular person confronting us. This realism is essential to our task. But it is not enough. We must also have the imaginative flair which allows us to understand this 'educating' from the side of the pupil, and helps him or her to divine the possibilities which are potentially present in every pupil and the secret which will release these. This combination of realism and imagination is the specific power of the educator.

This power is given a special name by Buber in which he combines both its elements. He calls it *Realphantasie* in German. This word has been variously translated as 'realistic imagination' and 'real fantasy' but neither of these do justice to the full import of the German word, which is as original as the capacity it was commandeered to describe. It means that the reality of 'inclusion', which must be present in every form of 'I-Thou' relationship, and which is present in its full concrete mutuality in the dialogue of friendship, is also present in the educational relation, but in a special way. It is not there in the symmetrical mutuality of friendship. The response from the pupil is other than that of the teacher. The teacher is present as he or she would be in a relation of friendship, but there is more involved here. Whatever is lacking from the pupil's side has to be supplemented by the teacher. 'Realistic imagination' allows the teacher to work the relationship also from the pupil's side, as though this latter were a somewhat paralyzed limb that had to be supported, until the strength of the relation grows to maturity and the teacher can withdraw this educative subvention. It is this 'supreme artistry of the teacher' which sees the full being of the child, recognizes what stands between the child and this fullness, and knows the secret of how to remove these obstacles. There are two ways we can influence the minds and the lives of others: by propaganda or by education. The first is the way of monologue in which 'one imposes one's opinion and attitude on the other in such a way that their psychic action is really one's own'. The second is the paradoxical reality of dialogical education, which is that 'legitimate influence' whereby one can release in the other their own capacity to release themselves.

This means, for Buber, that the teacher is required to release the 'Thou' in the pupil, without thereby either exploiting or fulfilling it. A genuine teacher has to be motivated by the one desire to release real being without seeking to enjoy it or appropriate it. Teachers have to invent the way, in this particular case and in the face of this concrete reality, of leading the child from individual monologue to personal dialogue.

This misunderstood notion of 'inclusion' represents one of the major contributions of Buber to educational philosophy. For our purposes here, it is important to understand both the difference and the similarity between the dialogue of friendship and the dialogue of education. Both are 'I-Thou' relationships, but the second belongs to the category of 'healing through meeting' and is a lesser form of the first, which can be understood as the fullest and most perfect form of dialogue. Both what they have in common and what differentiates them is the quality of the elements of 'inclusion', which defines, for Buber, the essence of any such relationship of dialogue. Education contains this element in a lesser and asymmetrical form, which results from the inequality of the partners in this relationship at the level of maturity of being and the fullness of personhood.

Both the dialogue of friendship and the dialogue of education are, for Buber, critical and liberating. There has been a tendency to misinterpret his notion of 'inclusion' and to reduce it to the more 'popular' notion of 'empathy'. Buber explicitly denies the connection between these two different ideas:[16]

> It would be wrong to identify what is meant here with the familiar but not very significant term 'empathy'. Empathy means, if anything, to glide with one's own feeling into the dynamic structure of an object ... and, as it were, to trace it from within, understanding the formation and motoriality of the object with the perceptions of one's own muscles; it means to 'transpose' oneself over there and in there. Thus it means the exclusion of one's own concreteness, the extinguishing of the actual situation of life, the absorption in pure aestheticism of the reality in which one participates. Inclusion is the opposite of this. It is the extension of one's own concreteness, the fulfillment of the actual situation of life, the complete presence of the reality in which one participates.

Dialogue, as 'inclusion', is the extension of a relationship between two equal and independent people. It does not mean that I abdicate my own identity in favour of some horizontal and unanchored link of feeling which would connect me to the other, regardless of any differences between us. Empathy requires no critical evaluation or open-eyed confirmation of the real being of the other, it substitutes for this an unqualified and sensitive acceptance of the other. Whatever truth or reality is attached to the being or presence of the other must be accepted and condoned in the empathic encounter. Such indiscriminate 'unity' is the search, not for confirmation and critical liberating dialogue, but for an ally or an accomplice. Empathy demands that the partner show no reaction other than sensitive and sympathetic understanding, without any reference to the objective or concrete justice or truth of the presence thus proferred.

By making an essential distinction between 'acceptance' and 'confirmation', Buber is asserting that an anchorless relationship of empathy, in which no exigence is imposed other than that of understanding the present situation of the 'other', is not enough to fulfill real relationship or genuine dialogue. There is the 'potentiality' of the person which must be honoured, even if this means refusing to confirm the present state of the other. There is also the fact of existence, the common ground of truth, an objective reality, which cannot be gainsaid in favor of some private world, made up of, and understood by, the two people who are interrelating:[17]

> I would say that every true existential relationship between two persons begins with acceptance. By acceptance I mean being able to tell, or rather not to tell, but only to make it felt to the other person, that I accept him as he is. I take you just as you are. Well, so, but it is not yet what I mean by confirming the other. Because accepting this is just accepting how he is at this moment, in this actuality of his. Confirming means first of all, accepting the whole potentiality of the other and making even a decisive difference in his potentiality ... I can recognize in him, know in him, more or less, the person

he has been (I can say it only in this word) *created* to become ... This is what we must, as far as we can, grasp, if not in the first moment, then after this. And now I not only accept the other as he is, but I confirm him, in myself, and then in him, in relation to this potentiality that is meant by him and it can now be developed ... Let's take for example, man and wife. He says to her, 'I accept you as you are'. But this does *not* mean, 'I don't want you to change'. Rather it says, 'Just by my accepting love, I discover in you what you are meant to become'.

So far, we have dealt with only two of the three forms of human dialogue enumerated by Buber. Friendship has been the fullest and most representative form of dialogue and we have shown the specific nature of educational dialogue by comparing it with and differentiating it from this paradigmatic form. In so doing, we have tried to describe the subtle and specific notion of 'inclusion' which defines both these relationships and to distinguish it from another, less subtle and ambiguous notion of empathy. All this is important in the context of ecumenical dialogue, where a dialogue of empathy would be entirely inappropriate.

However, before applying the analyses of this chapter to the sphere of ecumenism, and trying to establish whether the notion of dialogue as proposed by the Roman Catholic Church might be understood in terms of the dialogue of friendship or the dialogue of education, one last important distinction and criticism must be advanced.

Buber has been criticized for using the paradigm of the relationship of friendship as the essential one for explaining the reality of dialogue in general. His critics here would hold that friendship is a gift which mostly occurs between privileged people who form a kind of elite or aristocracy of the spirit. Such an experience, which may be possible for a very small percentage of the world's population, who have both the time and the means to cultivate such luxuries, can hardly be held up as an example for the way in which the common lot of humanity should enter into relationship with each other. Proposing such ethereal exercises as fundamental to the achievement of personhood seems to these critics to be almost as esoteric as suggesting that one cannot be fully human unless one can appreciate ballet, or cricket, or classical music. It divides the world into those capable and those incapable of such pursuits and it allows the latter to indulge in the erroneous belief that this 'work' of 'I-Thou' is promoting the destiny of mankind instead of being just the aesthetic pursuit of a superior handful. Buber answers such a critic in the following way:[18]

> (He) errs in a strange way when he supposes that I see in the *amitié toute spirituelle* the peak of the I-Thou relation. On the contrary, this relationship seems to me to win its true greatness and powerfulness precisely there where two men without a strong spiritual ground in common, even of very different kinds of spirit, yes of opposite dispositions, still stand over against each other so that each of the two knows and means, recognizes and acknowledges, accepts and confirms the other, even in the severest conflict, as this particular person. In the common situation of fighting with each other, he holds present to himself the experience-side of the other, his living through this situation. This is no friendship, this is only the comradeship of the human creature, a comradeship that has reached fulfillment.

This kind of dialogue is not the concrete mutuality of either friendship or education, it is what Buber calls the 'abstract' dialogue which has no other grounding in the 'between' than 'the hard human earth, the common in the uncommon'. However, it is in this abstract dialogue that 'the true greatness and powerfulness' of the 'I-Thou' relationship is to be found. It is here that it reaches its peak. An example of such dialogue is given by one of Buber's disciples, Aubrey Hodes. It forms the substance of one chapter in his book *Encounter with Martin Buber* called 'The Test'. The event takes place while Hodes, a Jew, was in medical service during the 1956 invasion of Egypt by Israel:[19]

> I was standing in front of the ambulance sorting out bottles and bandages when I saw a man in front of a prickly-pear hedge about twenty yards away. He was about sixty, fat and partly bald, in a filthy white shirt and torn khaki trousers, a civilian Arab. He took one hesitant, groping step from the hedge towards me, rolling his brown-stained eyes in terror, ready to draw back if I lifted my hand. Another step, and I saw that one arm hung in front of him with blood seeping through the piece of cheap colored cloth tied around it.
>
> Now he was coming slowly, like a crippled crab, towards the ambulance. Suddenly he made a desperate rush towards me and flung himself full length on the wooden bench in the shade of the olive trees.
>
> I looked at his arm. It had been broken, probably when we shelled the town, and it was starting to suppurate and smell in the midday heat. He turned his eyes to me as a puppy might have and held out his arm, which was trembling. I remember that the only word he said was *enta*, 'you'. He said this several times, like a child learning grammar, looking at me to see what I was going to do. Then he seemed to have decided that he could do nothing more. He closed his eyes and lay on the bench shaking and sweating.

The author bandaged his arm as best he could and describes that, while he was doing so, he did not think of the man as an Arab, belonging to the town and country they had occupied:

There was nothing noble or heroic about the act itself. The heat, the sticky red glue on the skin, his cotton white face and staccato chanting made it a human occasion forced on both of us by need, pain and accident.

When he had finished, two young soldiers from the unit arrived.

They saw the Arab and tried to drag him off and shoot him as an enemy. The author pushed the Arab into an ambulance and defended the door against the two young soldiers. They went to fetch the sergeant who threatened a court martial unless the prisoner were turned over to him immediately. The author refused and when the three had departed, he let the Arab out of the ambulance and set him free. Hodes then tells how he later related the incident to Buber:

> I went to see Buber at his home in Jerusalem ... I told him about the incident in Khan Yunis; about the Moroccan boys and the sergeant, about the Arab who had been sent in my path ... Buber listened intently, focusing on every word. When I described the two young Moroccans bursting on to the scene he closed his eyes in pain. I came to the end and stopped. Telling it was harder than living through it had been. I wondered about the old Arab and if he'd got away.
>
> Buber leaned forward and gave me a long intense look. In it I saw pride, love, trust. I had never heard his voice so tender. 'You have passed your test', he said.

Such an example of dialogue should offset any attempt to reduce the 'I-Thou' relationship to a privileged intimacy between the spiritually gifted. It also completes our survey of the three kinds of inter-human dialogue described by Buber.

Although it is true that the relationship of friendship does mark the fullness and the perfection of the life of dialogue 'being based on a concrete and mutual experience of inclusion' which is 'the true inclusion of one another by human souls',[20] it cannot by identified with such life. 'It is a grace for which one must always be ready and which one never gains as an assured possession'.[21] Besides this perfection which occurs as a grace and a gift, and which probably is the one which makes the whole life of dialogue seem worthwhile, there is also the 'abstract' form of dialogue where the partners, 'although thoroughly different in nature and outlook', are still 'aware of the other's full legitimacy'.[22] Here the mutuality and inclusion which must make up any 'I-Thou' relationship, extend to both partners only as 'spiritual persons' and leave out the full reality of their being and life. It is in this second form that the life of dialogue shows its greatness and its powerfulness, requiring the most effort and generosity on the part of both partners.

The third form of dialogical relation describes 'those I-Thou relationships which in their nature may not unfold to full mutuality if they are to persist in that nature'.[23] It is described by Buber as 'the relation of education', but it could be extended to include any form of therapeutic relationship and need not necessarily be confined to the relationship between a teacher and a pupil. It is based upon 'a concrete but one-sided experience of inclusion'.[24] This survey of all three forms of dialogue should have shown that the basic attitude of 'I-Thou' is divided into an abstract and a concrete form. The concrete form is further divided into a two-sided experience of inclusion which is the relationship of friendship, and a one-sided experience of inclusion which Buber calls the educational relation. All these forms have common characteristics which unite them under the generic heading of I-Thou relationships, and each one has specific characteristics which separate them into different 'forms' within this basic category.

In the next chapter these analyses will be applied to the different forms of ecumenical dialogue within the framework of the Roman Catholic Church, in the hope that such an application may clarify some issues and make it possible to decide whether our dialogical relations with non-Christians takes the 'abstract' form and whether our dialogue with our fellow Christians is to be characterized in similar terms or in the modality of friendship or education.

Notes

1   Martin Buber, *The Knowledge of Man* (London, 1965), p. 64.
2   Ibid., pp. 12-13.
3   Martin Buber, *Between Man and Man* (Collins, Glasgow, 1979), pp. 27-28.
4   Ibid., pp. 53-54.
5   Ibid., p. 59.
6   Ibid., p. 57.
7   Ibid., p. 40.
8   Martin Buber, *I and Thou*, New York, 1960, p. 11.
9   Martin Buber, *Between Man and Man*, op. cit., p. 125.
10   Ibid.
11   Ibid.
12   Martin Buber, *The Knowledge of Man*, (London, 1965), p. 68
13   Aubrey Hodes, *Encounter with Martin Buber* (Penguin, 1975), p. 138.
14   Martin Buber, *Between Man and Man*, op. cit., p. 126.
15   Ibid., p. 128.
16   Ibid., p. 124.
17   Martin Buber, *The Knowledge of Man*, (London, 1965), p. 181.
18   *The Philosophy of Martin Buber*, op. cit., pp. 723-724.
19   Aubrey Hodes, *Encounter with Martin Buber* (Penguin, 1975), p. 48.
20   Martin Buber, *Between Man and Man*, op. cit., p. 128.
21   Martin Buber, *I and Thou*, op. cit., p. 131.
22   Martin Buber, *Between Man and Man*, op. cit., p. 126.
23   Martin Buber, *I and Thou*, op. cit., p. 131.
24   Martin Buber, *Between Man and Man*, op. cit., p. 127.

CHAPTER IV

WHAT DO WE MEAN BY DIALOGUE?

The question is whether the theology of the Roman Catholic Church can allow its members to engage in genuine dialogue and, if so, what form and direction that dialogue should take?

To answer this question, or, at least to try to clarify the issues involved, an attempt will be made in this chapter to superimpose the findings of the first two chapters upon the structure outlined in the third. This will, at least, allow for some assessment of this nebulous term 'dialogue' when it is used in the context of ecumenism. Obviously, there is no intention here of suggesting either that Martin Buber has said the last word about dialogue, or that the very cursory summary of his thought on this matter given in the last chapter has said the last word about Martin Buber. The purpose of this exercise is to present a model of dialogue, as this word is explained in one particular philosophical vocabulary, which will help to clarify what the Church means when it brings this word into such prominence in its teaching during and since the second Vatican Council.

Dialogue is a word which has a precise and definite meaning in the language of some and a vague though benevolent connotation in the language of others. For some it could be as old, as wide and as mandatory as that 'charity' which describes

Christianity and at the same time says nothing at all about it. It's just a new word for love, which appeals to the people of our generation. In this way, the term is robbed of any originality or any danger. It is just what we have always been doing and preaching from the very beginning, and if modern youth or anyone else have to call it something else to make it more digestible, then we will condescendingly comply. After all, a rose by any other name… Thus, when the Council documents urge us to have dialogue with our separated Christian brethren and those who do not profess any belief in the divinity of Christ, no change of attitude or alteration of approach is indicated, because we have been urged to do this since the foundation of Christianity. The vocabulary of the Council is, in this view, old wine in new skins.

Such vague and benign platitudes are not what other more rigorous and demanding interpreters expect. And forty years after the council, when the Church has been using this term in nearly every official document issuing from the Vatican until it has almost become an overused cliché, it is important that some cogent and authoritative statement be made about the precise meaning of this term in Roman Catholic Theology. The purpose of this presentation of the problem is obviously not to make such a statement. It is simply to lessen the ambiguity by showing what one modern philosopher means when he uses this term. Martin Buber's notion of dialogue may not be comprehensive or definitive, but it is, at least, a respectable attempt to clarify the possible meaning of this fashionable and optimistic notion. It provides a yardstick and a focal point from which it is possible to chart a course, either in agreement or in opposition, towards a more coherent use of the word dialogue in our theological vocabulary.

I. Separation

The first point which was made in our presentation of Buber's thought was that all dialogue presupposes the fundamental reality of distance or separation. This primal distance, at the ontological level, describes the fact that each one of us is a separate and distinct entity and that this essential difference has to be accomplished before any relation of dialogue can be established. At the ecclesiastical level, this reality of distance or separation would mean the marking out of the boundaries between the Roman Catholic Church and all the others who do not belong to this particular identifiable reality. Such a setting at a distance requires two exercises in definition. The first is an understanding of the precise and defining reality of the Church itself. The second is a mapping out of the quality and the quantity of distance which separates this reality from all the other distinguishable realities defined by their particular religious denomination, which share with us the universe in which we live.

The defining element of the first reality is the ontological imparting of the divine life of the one true God to those who are baptized into the Christian Church. This ontological stamp is what marks off the boundaries between this Church and the rest of the world. If we believe that the divine life is shared only and exclusively through the mediation of our particular Church structure, then the distance between us and every other human being in the world is an unbridgeable one between being and non-being. In such a view there can be no dialogue between us and these others as Christians or as equals. Every dialogue is a relation and relation is, of its essence, established between two terms. In this case the 'other' has no existence, no reality, and cannot, therefore, draw from within itself the elements necessary to make it into a partner in dialogue. It may have been possible to hold this view in other eras of history. Some might claim that until the Second Vatican Council, certain Roman Catholics were justified in maintaining such a position. The theological slogan that 'outside the Church there is no salvation', however qualified and nuanced it may have been in the thought of those Church Fathers from whom it derives its origin, came to be interpreted by the more simple and less subtle as meaning that no real presence of God was possible outside the official channels of the Catholic Church.

Presumably, also, there were times in the history of civilization when it did seem possible that membership of this one organ of divine presence would be a tangible reality for every human being inhabiting the known universe. The missionary activity of the Church would take on an urgent and global dimension under such circumstances, and respect for human freedom and difference would take second place to the huge responsibility imposed upon the Church to see that as many as possible availed of this unique offer. In such a perspective there can be no acceptance of the reality of separation. The Church's understanding of herself could be described as totalitarian and her relationship with all those outside the one true fold, colonial. There can be no question of establishing a relationship with other people or religions as partners in dialogue. There is only one reality, one truth, which has the right and the duty to extend itself to the ends of the earth, until it either crushes or absorbs all that steps up to meet it in the way. Such a vision would go a long way towards explaining such historical realities as the cruel conquests by the Christian nations of the 'new' world and such otherwise incomprehensible notorieties as the 'Inquisition'.

However, as the world continued to increase and the Christian Empire to decline steadily, it became apparent that such totalitarian dreams were simply not going to be realized. This *fait accompli* gave rise to another theological viewpoint, which was one of the same ilk but slightly more adapted to the statistics of the case. This second formula found biblical sustenance in the theme of 'the remnant of Israel', that small band of the elect, who certainly take up a very creditable proportion of Old Testament ecclesiology.

Such an adapted version of the same theme would present the Catholic Church as an exclusive minority in an increasingly secular and irreligious world. The important thing for this small band of the elect to do was to maintain its integrity and bide its time until the world was brought to realize that it alone possessed the truth for which humankind was secretly yearning. When the time was ripe and the Lord of all the ages decided to visit his wrath upon all those who had refused to accept his offer of salvation, definitively incarnated in and institutionalized by the Roman Catholic Church, then this faithful remnant would step forth to announce to the world the truth which it had held intact from the foundations of Christianity. However, the important question for Roman Catholics was: 'When the Son of Man returns, will he still find faith on earth?' Would the small band of the elect have remained faithful to His teaching and preserved it untarnished by the multiple aberrations of heretics and false prophets?

Such a strategy, although less strident and triumphalist, is similar in kind to the totalitarian view. The difference between the two is simply one of attitude. The exclusivist theology tended to inculcate an introspective and fearful ghetto mentality, over-scrupulous about the letter of the law and almost pathologically fearful of contamination from 'the world'.

One of the inherent weaknesses of these two refusals to accept the fundamental fact of 'separation' between Christians and 'others' in the world, and their corresponding corollaries of either totalitarianism or exclusivism, depending upon the historical and political situation of the time, is that they imply a unity and unanimity about the truth within the phenomenon of Christianity itself. At the time of the Second Vatican Council, it was not only clear that the minority status of Christianity as a whole within the totality of the world's population was allowing our period of world history to be called the 'post-Christian era' by some cultural commentators, but it was also clear that there were seemingly irreconcilable divisions between the different Churches which made up the steadily dwindling Christian minority. Statistics of the time recorded that there were about 540,000,000 Roman Catholics, 215,000,000 Protestants and 130,000,000 Orthodox Christians, each claiming ownership of the truth which Christ had revealed to the world.

Without going into the details of the various historical situations which brought about these divisions, it could be said that the disunity of Christendom took place in three main stages. In the fifth century there was the separation of the Nestorian and Monophysite Churches in the East from the Byzantine Church of Rome and Constantinople. By the eleventh century the incipient rift between Rome and Constantinople (which then included the more recent Churches of Russia, Bulgaria, Serbia and others) had become an explicit and definitive separation. Finally, within the Roman Catholic Church itself, the sixteenth century produced the schism between this Church and the various Protestant bodies which separated themselves from it.

It is probably true to say that the occasion of the Second Vatican Council was one which allowed the assembled bishops to understand in a practical and concrete way what the actual situation of the Roman Catholic Church was in terms of the total spectrum of the world's population and its variety of religious affiliation. Up to that time each bishop faced the particular concrete situation of his own diocese in his own country. No one diocese included all the tensions generated by the presence of all these differences, whether inside or outside the realms of Christianity.

In Ireland, for instance, the practical problems of ecclesiastical life were almost reduced to the third stage of Christian disunity, the differences between Roman Catholics and Protestants. It was possible for Irish Roman Catholics to be totally unaware of the reality of atheism, the religions of Islam or Hinduism, for example, or even, within the confines of Christianity, of either the existence or the claims of the

Orthodox Church. The experience of the Second Vatican Council was one which allowed us to understand more fully the reality of 'separation' in all its directions, its depth and its plurality of form.

II.   Monologue.

Having established the fact of separation as a reality which constitutes the ecclesial situation, the next step is to elaborate the primary gesture of the Church within this situation; is it to be a monologue or a dialogue in Buber's terms?

As we have seen, monologue is, in fact, a kind of relation. It is not to be confused with non-relation. It means that the Catholic Church accepts the fact of separation or distance, but, instead of closing itself off from all those who are not its members, it opens itself out to all the world in readiness to share its riches with all those who have ears to hear with. The relationship here is entirely one-sided. The Church has absolutely nothing to learn from these outsiders who surround her. She may listen to them, but not to learn from them, rather the better to teach them what she alone knows. Many would certainly claim that this monological relationship with all non-Catholics was the one adopted by the Roman Catholic Church before Vatican II. Such a relationship could also be classified as 'apostolic' or 'apologetic' and would be regarded by Buber as below the threshold of genuine dialogue. The question we have to ask ourselves is whether the Decree on Ecumenism and the teaching of the Church since its promulgation allow us to claim that a change has taken place and that we have, in fact, adopted a dialogical stance.

In this regard it is interesting to read some of the literature about ecumenism which predates the Vatican Council. One such text was written by Gustave Weigel SJ in 1960:[1]

> The Roman Catholic Church (and therefore each Catholic to the degree in which he is assimilated into the genuine life and being of his Church) believes that this

Church is exclusively the Church of Christ. By that fact she believes that she is Christ continued in space and time, with His mission to save, to teach, to judge, to comfort, to guide, to sanctify, and all this she will do because Christ and Catholicism are fused into one life with Him as head and she as the body. Because she believes that His name saves and in no other name is there salvation, she conceives of herself as the saving instrument of God for men, and in her view there is no other. She well knows that God in his soul-loving benevolence also brings men who are non-Catholic to a happy term by uncovenanted mercies. But in this saving act, such souls are attached invisibly to the visible Church. We cannot call them members, but they are truly adherents... It is God aiding His Church in her mission to save souls. But no other instrument is ordained by God to dispense grace to mankind.

This is the theory and spirit of Catholicism. It may appear utterly preposterous to a non-Catholic, but there it is. Psychologically and logically the Roman Catholic Church simply cannot conceive of any other human union as ordained by God to mediate salvation, even though individual members of such a union be in grace. Such grace is immediately given by God in favour of this individual.

This is the logic and the psychology of monologue. I give this quotation, not as a unique or even unusual expression of the Roman Catholic position prior to Vatican II, it could be paralleled and multiplied by many other examples. In fact, for the time, it represents a more open approach than other theologians would have provided. I give it also because the book in which it appears carries on the dust-cover a highly significant comment from a well known ecumenist George H. Tavard, who writes that this statement of the Catholic position on ecumenism 'is a valuable contribution to the development of a far-reaching dialogue among Christians ... Fr Weigel is one of our most persuasive promoters of ecumenical good will'.

To show just how much ground has been covered and how much higher are ecumenical expectations in the years after the Vatican Council, here is a quote from an article by that same George H. Tavard written in 1979:[2]

> Dialogue has been described rather well, in the Decree on Ecumenism of the Second Vatican Council, as involving two or more Churches which have agreed to talk together *par cum pari*. In the text of the decree, this expression applies directly to individual participants in ecumenical conversations. But insofar as these represent their Churches, it is the Churches themselves which, through the participants, meet and talk *par cum pari*. As I understand it, this implies that each side considers the other, at least tentatively, as of equal value. That is, it agrees to make the hypothesis of the other's formulation of faith or theology; to try and enter as deeply as possible into the mindset of the other side, a mindset which precisely makes another formulation of faith, another theology possible, consistent and, in its context and limits, faithful to the gospel. At the limit, each side agrees to consider the formulation of faith of the other side as valid alternative to its own. At this level, one is no longer in apologetics, or even in comparative theology and ecclesiology; one is caught in a process of convergence, in an attempt to build together a theology which will do justice to the history and the insights of both sides. Such a theology will be new in relation to all the past theologies of the Churches engaged in dialogue.
>
> In terms of theology as language, this means that dialogue obliges each side to adopt a very flexible view of the theology which serves as its point of departure.

Theology can no longer be a synchronic synthesis elaborated at what we may like to see as the high point of our own Church's intellectual development. Such a synchronic synthesis and other such elaborations now become historical moments in an on-going movement of which the present dialogue constitutes another moment. And the *kairos* of this dialogical moment resides exactly in the opportunity to enrich one theological language by another, through modification of its paradigms, of its method (grammar), of its formulation of the Mystery in the light and with the help of the paradigms, the method, the formulation of the Mystery of the other Church with which we are dialoguing.

This somewhat lengthy quotation is necessary to show what one ecumenical commentator, who has studied the position of the Roman Catholic Church for many years, has been led to expect from that Church in terms of dialogue, by his reading of the text 'On Ecumenism' of the Second Vatican Council. And this is no naïve or over-enthusiastic newcomer to the field. As we have seen from his comments quoted above, he is quite prepared to accept the position of the Catholic Church as outlined by Gustave Weigel in 1960, even though this position must, by self-definition, exclude the possibility of genuine dialogue. However, he is convinced, rightly or wrongly, that the Church's teaching of the Second Vatican Council has changed all that and that she is now in a theological position to make the reality of dialogue possible.

The important issue from our point of view is to clarify the ambiguity generated by this document on ecumenism and, indeed, by the whole phenomenon of the Second Vatican Council. There is no doubt that the interpretation of dialogue, as this is described in the Decree on Ecumenism, contained in the second quotation given above, would qualify for the fullest kind of dialogue as this is presented in the theory of Martin

Buber. And so, it is true that the teaching of Vatican II is capable of allowing some, both inside and outside the Church, to imagine that a great change has taken place in the Roman Catholic Church's self-definition and that after this council the genuine reality of dialogue became possible for the first time. Now, from our point of view, it is very far from clear whether:

a) this description of dialogue, offered by George Tavard, could be taken as a fair representation of the teaching of the Decree on Ecumenism.
b) the Catholic Church could ever accept such a definition of dialogue as consistent with her own understanding of herself and of the responsibilities and obligations laid upon her by the burden of that self-understanding.

It is neither the purpose nor within the power of a book like this to answer these questions. The purpose here is to clarify the issues and work towards receiving some official theology of dialogue. It is unfair to members of our own Church and to all those potential partners in dialogue to allow such ambiguity to continue forty years after the event. If it is not true that the full reality of genuine dialogue is open to Roman Catholics, then it is time to say this unambiguously.

Whatever about the exact definition of the term 'dialogue', it seems clear that the Second Vatican Council did finally commit the Roman Catholic Church to this path in such a way that it is no longer possible for any of its members to understand its position vis-à-vis the other Christian Churches in terms of monologue as this term is described by Buber. The 'monological' attitude may have been possible to defend and to adopt prior to this Council, but since then this is no longer the case.

The three most fundamental statements issued by that Council, which made a 'monological' attitude impossible from that time onwards were the declaration on Religious Liberty, the definition of the Catholic Church in terms of truth as found in the decree *Lumen Gentium* and the admission that Churches other than the Roman Catholic can be channels of divine grace, which is stated in the Decree on Ecumenism.

The first of these points is contained in the following quotation from the Decree on Religious Liberty:[3]

> The Vatican Council declares that the human person has a right to religious freedom. Freedom of this kind means that all men should be immune from coercion on the part of individuals, social groups and every human power so that, within due limits, nobody is forced to act against his convictions nor is anyone to be restrained from acting in accordance with his convictions in religious matters in private or in public, alone or in associations with others. The Council further declares that the right to religious freedom is based on the very dignity of the human person as known through the revealed word of God and by reason itself. This right of the human person to religious freedom must be given such recognition in the constitutional order of society as will make it a civil right.

Now, although this may sound banal and obvious to a reader in the twenty-first century, it was a very important statement for the Catholic Church to have made and it certainly gives no further grounds for the totalitarian attitude of former centuries, based on the notion that 'error has no rights'. The statement could hardly be hailed as a milestone in human history and it must be said that the Catholic Church is rather late in officially endorsing the principle of human freedom in December 1965, when it was already recognized by constitutional law even to the point that those of the Marxist-Leninist political ideology were forced to pay at least lip-service to it, however, it was a welcome clarification of an essential principle. In the past it was possible for the Church to maintain something of a double standard when dealing with the powers of the secular order: freedom for the Church in those countries where Catholics were in the minority, but privilege for the Church and intolerance towards others in those situations where Catholics were in the majority. This declaration on religious freedom definitively overrules any such ambiguity. It must also be said that this statement has the effect of retrospectively condemning as an obvious evil the various religious wars of the Middle Ages, in which several Catholic prelates and a number of popes took part.

The second point is really contained in one sentence from the Decree on the Church, *Lumen Gentium*, which one theologian has described as the crowbar to the wall of exclusivism:[4]

> The one mediator, Christ, established and ever sustains here on earth his holy Church, the community of faith, hope and charity, as a visible organization through which he communicates truth and grace to all men ... This is the sole Church of Christ which in the Creed we profess to be one, holy, catholic and apostolic, which our Saviour, after his resurrection, entrusted to Peter's pastoral care (Jn. 21:17), commissioning him and the other apostles to extend and rule it (cf. Matt. 28:18, etc.), and which he raised up for all ages as 'the pillar and mainstay of the truth' (1 Tim. 3:15). This Church, constituted and organized as a society in the present world, subsists in the Catholic Church, which is governed by the successor of Peter and by the bishops in communion with him. Nevertheless, many elements of sanctification and of truth are found outside its visible confines. Since these are gifts belonging to the Church of Christ, they are forces impelling towards Catholic unity.

It is the second last sentence in this paragraph which changes the tone of the Church's self-understanding. The words 'subsists in' (*subsistit*) replaced the word 'is' (*est*) in the original text and, although somewhat vague in their precise meaning, prevent us from ever again identifying the Roman Catholic Church exclusively with the one, holy, catholic and apostolic Church founded by Christ.

The third point can be seen as a corollary to the above and is to be found in the Decree on Ecumenism: [5]

> In this one and only Church of God from its very beginnings there arose certain rifts, which the Apostle strongly censures as damnable. But in subsequent centuries much more serious dissentions appeared and large communities became separated from full communion with the Catholic Church – for which, often enough, men of both sides were to blame. However, one cannot charge with the sin of separation those who at present are born into these communities and in them are brought up in the faith of Christ, and the Catholic Church accepts them with respect and affection as brothers. For men who believe in Christ and have been properly baptized are put in some, though imperfect, communion with the Catholic Church … But … it remains true that all those who have been justified by faith in baptism are incorporated into Christ; they therefore have a right to be called Christians, and with good reason are accepted as brothers by the children of the Catholic Church.
>
> Moreover, some, even very many, of the most significant elements and endowments which together go to build up and give life to the Church itself, can exist outside the visible boundaries of the Catholic Church: the written Word of God; the life of Grace; faith, hope and charity, with the other interior gifts of the Holy Spirit, as well as visible elements.

All of these, which come from Christ and lead back to him, belong by right to the one Church of Christ.

The brethren divided from us also carry out many liturgical actions of the Christian religion. In ways that vary according to the condition of each Church or community, these liturgical actions most certainly can truly engender a life of grace, and, one must say, can aptly give access to the communion of salvation.

In this and similar statements of the Vatican Council, the Church has come a long way from the notion that she alone is exclusively the Church of Christ, that she is the only saving instrument of God for humanity and that no other instrument is ordained by God to dispense grace to humankind.

In this context it becomes clear that even if the monological relationship between the Church and other, non-Catholic people may have been a possibility in the past, this can no longer be the case. The Catholic Church is, from her very situation in the world, by definition, a Church of dialogue. Not only does her apostolic mission impel her to be so, but her very integrity demands that she achieve the unity which was the explicit prayer of her founder. The fact that she now admits some blame for the scandalous divisions which have occurred, and that she accepts that other Churches contain within their visible structures something of that divine life which Christ came on earth to establish among us, means that it is at her own peril that she cuts herself off completely from these other sources of unity and grace.

And so it seems clear that, at least since the Second Vatican Council, the Roman Catholic Church is committed to the way of dialogue, if not with all people, at least with the other Christian denominations, although it is still not clear what that way of dialogue either demands or implies.

III.   Dialogue

Having established both the fact of separation and the way of dialogue as the relationship appropriate to that separation, it remains now to tease out the exact form of that dialogue within the different situations in which the Church finds itself. Once again it may be useful to take the analyses of Martin Buber as our guide and to apply these to the various forms of dialogue which make up the spectrum of our various kinds of relationships with non-Catholics.

In the tabulation of the various kinds of dialogue outlined by Buber, it might be interesting to examine the relationship between the Church and the non-Christian world in terms of the 'abstract' form of dialogue described in Chapter Three. However, the purpose of this book is to try to clarify the kind of dialogue which should exist between Roman Catholics and those other Churches which profess belief in Christ. In this context it seems clear that, if we take Buber's outline as our model, we are dealing here with the realm of 'concrete' dialogue, sharing as we do the common ground of belief in Christ, the written word of the New Testament, belief in the working of the Holy Spirit within our liturgical assemblies and in the inner life of each individual believer.

Taking this common 'concrete' ground as our starting-point, we can narrow down the possibilities to the two forms which Buber calls the dialogue of friendship and the dialogue of education. Whether we decide to opt for the one or the other, it is important to remember the twofold essence of any relationship of dialogue in whatever form it takes: the notion of 'inclusion' with its double exigence of 'acceptance' and 'confirmation'. There can be no question here of a false irenicism which would water down the principles or the demands of each denomination to achieve a unity at all costs, based on the lowest common denominator of dogmatic formulae acceptable to all those participating in the dialogue.

Although the basis of all dialogue is an acceptance of and a respect for the reality and the integrity of the 'other' as that other actually is, this is not the only constitutive element, nor is it the full meaning of either educational dialogue or the dialogue of friendship. The equally important element of 'confirmation' demands that we also respect the potentiality for growth in the other, the fuller reality that this other might be called to grow towards; our own potentiality for growth and a fuller reality which we might be called to; and that such growth might not even become apparent until after our dialogue has begun. There are very deep and sometimes incompatible differences of a fundamental nature between the various Christian denominations. These cannot be watered down or hidden away. They must be brought to the relationship and presented fully and coherently with trust and humility. To predict what the outcome of such dialogue might be would depend entirely upon whether we understand our dialogue as one of friendship or of education. If it is the first, then we accept the equal status and validity of the other point of view and are open to the mutual enrichment and growth which such shared reciprocity must bring, through the working of the Holy Spirit, without staking out beforehand the boundaries beyond which we are not prepared to go; if it is the second, then we enter the dialogue in the belief that both we and our partners will be brought, by the light of the Holy Spirit, to that fullness of Christianity, which we are confident exists, in however obscure a shape, within the boundaries of the Roman Catholic Church as she is presently constituted. In other words, the dialogue of friendship exists between partners who are fully mature and responsible Christians seeking to enrich each other by mutual and reciprocal sharing of the graces they have received, whereas the dialogue of education exists between one mature partner and others who have not yet either experienced or realized the full potentiality of their being in Christ.

A close reading of the encyclical *Ecclesiam Suam* and an elucidation of that text called 'Dialogue on Dialogue' in which it is discussed in a conversation between Paul VI and Jean Guitton,[6] would seem to confirm that the notion of dialogue proposed here is close to, if not identical with, what Martin Buber would describe as 'educational' dialogue. The basic image of dialogue in terms of concentric circles surrounding the focus of the Roman Catholic Church which ends the encyclical and takes up much of the ensuing conversation, implies that there is only one axiological centre of Christianity from which all other Christians must be approached and defined. This presupposition also implies that the other Churches have no real 'being' within themselves and that 'dialogue' will reveal to them the true source of their being which is to be found in the Catholic Church as the archetype of what they are striving, even though, perhaps, unknowingly, to become. Guitton describes what dialogue means to Paul VI in the following way:[7]

> This word becomes with him a universal mirror-word, a sun, a pivot, a hinge, a spring, a focus, a mystery, a summation of thoughts, a world of possibilities ... It is a matter of seeking truth in the other and in oneself, of ceaselessly entering into contact with another mind, but one equally in love with truth, in its precision, its purity, I would say in its supreme subtlety ... It is a question of thinking in common, always ready to correct oneself by another's view; it is a question of being helped by one's adversary in the search for what *is*.

Guitton himself wrote an article in *La Croix* in which he tried to distinguish between the notion of 'dialogue' and the notion of 'dialectic', in which 'the creative intelligence is solitary and, like the spider, weaves its web' without according any reality to the 'other'. 'For dialogue', he concludes, 'being the confrontation by two friends of eternal truth, is a free exercise in which each swears to the other not to give way, except to the light.'[8] And he quotes Lacordaire as saying that 'I do not try to convince my adversary of error, but to join him in a higher truth'.

But as the conversation continues it becomes clear that there is a certain ambiguity about the meaning of the word 'equality', which both participants agree to be necessary for what they understand as 'dialogue'. Guitton asks how it is possible to achieve 'that equality which never exists among men'? The Pope suggests that this view means 'that no dialogue is possible between son and father, disciple and master; and, especially, between a layman and the Pope'. He claims that the 'equality' needed for dialogue is not provided by 'situation, information, authority, age, talent, not even by genius, but by an equal love of truth'. This absolute love of truth makes equal those who sincerely seek it together.

However, Guitton puts his finger immediately on the weakness and the ambiguity by asking: 'But when a believer has a dialogue with an atheist, where is the equality? One possesses, the other is dispossessed'. And here the Pope refers to the metaphor of concentric circles, or, as he calls them, 'zones of adhesion'. The first circle, the widest, includes all humanity; the second are those who believe in one sole God; the third are all those who have heard the call of Christ and who recognize him as God. And then, within the circle of Christians there are also circles. 'The Orthodox are very near to us. Our brothers of the Reform form a larger and more differentiated circle.' And the Pope would claim that 'between those who inhabit these different circles of thought and sincere conviction, there can be dialogue', but 'we at the centre have a duty … to be worthy of that central focus'. This demands of us 'never to mistake human obligations for divine exigencies' and it asks of those in the wider circles to question themselves about 'whether their faith is sufficiently developed, whether, in order to remain itself, it must not rise, *go up higher*. It is our conviction that they are not yet in their fullness'.

From the centre to the periphery there are two movements which Paul VI describes as like the two movements of breathing: the first goes from the world to the Church, from the periphery to the centre, and is 'animated by the just desire to understand the contemporary world, to accept its ways of living and feeling, to draw from life's experience a more human theology, to give Christianity new expression': the second movement goes from the Church to the world, from the centre to the periphery, and 'starts from the values deposited among the Church's treasure'. Here we must see how much of the divine truth the world can bear and, in this movement of dialogue, the Catholic partner 'adapts himself, as God does; he becomes an educator.'[9]

Although the Pope concedes that the first movement is the one which is more demanding and especially of love because 'it puts itself in modern man's place, it adopts his viewpoint, including, for example, his criticisms and disappointments with Christians, with Catholics', he still maintains that 'the truth of faith demands an entire, frank adhesion, no less today than yesterday and always'. 'Truth, his truth, is firm and sure. It is the exact reflection, even if for us an enigmatic one, of objective, wholesome reality. Time does not change or distort this truth, but commands and deepens it. History does not impair or destroy it; it changes neither its significance nor its value, but it develops it and applies it with wisdom to new conditions. Science, far from rendering it empty, seeks, implores it, in a sense. The Church keeps it, is worthy of it. The Church defends it, professes it, possesses it.'[10]

The dialogue envisaged here is that one-sided inclusion which takes place between two partners, one of whom is fully mature in being while the other has not yet fully realized full potential. The empathic movement from the centre to the periphery, which makes up an essential, but less important, element of this dialogue, is really little more than a human technique, a way of making it easier for the 'other' to reach the equality of full possession of divine truth. The 'other' in this dialogue is required, through it, to step upwards towards the light. Such a description fits perfectly the type of dialogue which Buber calls educational.

If the meaning of this term within the Catholic Church is to be identified with the explanation given of it by Pope Paul VI and if the definitive exegesis of the Second Vatican Council's Decree on Ecumenism is to be found in his previous encyclical *Ecclesiam Suam*, then it is important to say this authoritatively both to the members of the Roman Catholic Church and to those with whom we are engaged in ecumenical dialogue. Otherwise many illusions and false hopes can be, and have been, entertained both inside and outside the Catholic Church since the Decree was issued in 1964.

However, before definitively making such an identification of the Council Document and the papal encyclical and of the Church's teaching on dialogue and Martin Buber's notion of educational dialogue, it is important to examine one last possibility which could lead to a less rigid understanding of this term.

Is it not possible that the Roman Catholic Church is called to that fullest kind of dialogue which Buber would call the dialogue of friendship with those other Christian Churches that are not in full communion with Rome? An affirmative answer to this question would have to be based upon a differentiation between the unique event which was the Second Vatican Council and any elucidation, either before or afterwards, of the meaning of that event, and would have to take as its basic document the text of that Council on Ecumenism, rather than any previous or subsequent interpretation of that text.

Such an understanding would claim that the event which was the summoning and the actual working of that unique council was essentially the energy of the Holy Spirit, working, most obviously through the instrumentality of Pope John XXIII, and achieving results which went beyond anything that either the imagination or the audacity of any one particular participant would have foreseen or engineered. As we have seen from the first chapter, the text on ecumenism, despite the many human and material obstacles which stood in its way, emerged as something of a miracle, even if also as something of an enigma. Reading it now, forty years later, it appears, at times, to be somewhat obscure, if not ambiguous. This is both its strength and its weakness: strength in the richness of possibilities which it thus provides; weakness in the lack of any definitive textual backing for whatever interpretation theologians may later try to draw from it.

To make a case for what Buber would call the dialogue of friendship as the appropriate relationship between the Roman Catholic Church and the other Christian Churches we would have to see the document of the Second Vatican Council as the high-point of doctrinal statement on this matter. This would mean that the papal encyclical which predated it could not be taken as a definitive exegesis of this text. The text itself would be seen as a step forward from that encyclical and one that opened new horizons in the understanding of ecumenical dialogue.

Dialogue itself would be seen as something which has been revealed, not just to the Church, but to the whole of our world, as a new way of relating to each other, as a new way of being. This would obviously be attributable to the Holy Spirit, working in the world in the ubiquitous and unforeseen ways that are always open to this Spirit, but not, this time, working directly through the official channels of the Catholic Church. The work of that Church, under these circumstances, would be the exercise of that discernment of the Spirit which would allow such a charismatic figure as John XXIII to read the signs of the times and recognize the spiritual value of this way of relating to others.

Such a prompting of the Spirit would be connected to a whole movement in human understanding away from the technological world of our century and also away from the substantive mode of thinking which all of our culture inherited from Aristotle. It would be the result of a new awareness of the importance and the dignity of the human person and also the reinstating of the category of relation as the most fundamental one at the level of being in our Western metaphysics.

This, again, would make us rethink our concepts of truth. Just as we have seen that the old idea of truth having rights and error having no rights was dismissed because, as Cardinal Bea put it in a talk he gave at Pro Deo University in Rome on 13 January 1963, truth and error are both abstract concepts incapable of having either rights or obligations; so, it is possible to say that the essential 'truth' of the Christian faith is a guaranteed relationship with a person, and that a more correct way of stating that truth is to say that we are possessed by it rather than that we, or anyone else, possess it as an ascertainable object.

The change which was made in the Council document from 'Principles of Catholic Ecumenism' to 'Catholic Principles on Ecumenism' would suggest here that ecumenical dialogue was not something which belonged to the Catholic Church, but rather a reality to which the Catholic Church brought her own being and her own principles. The actual dialogue would then be seen as a common ground, a reality which all of us living in the twentieth and twenty-first centuries were called upon to enter into and respect. The fact that we recognize the Baptism of other Churches and the fact that these other Churches can be channels of divine life and grace, would also seem to point to an equality at the level of being which would give a very significant emphasis to the famous phrase *'par cum pari'*, by which we are enjoined to 'treat with the other on an equal footing'.

Notes

1   Gustave Weigel SJ, *Where we Differ?* (London, 1960), pp. 76-77.
2   George H. Tavard, 'For a Theology of Dialogue', *One in Christ* 1979, no 1, pp. 14-15.
3   Documents of *Vatican Council II* (ed. Flannery, 1981), p. 800.
4   Ibid., p. 357.
5   Ibid., p. 455.
6   Jean Guitton, *The Pope Speaks* (London 1968), pp. 161-182.
7   Ibid., pp. 162-3.
8   Ibid., p. 164.
9   Ibid., p. 179.
10 Ibid., p. 181.

CHAPTER V

BECAUSE WE ARE A DIALOGUE

We are only mouth. Who sings the distant heart
That dwells entire within all things?
Its great pulse lives in us
divided into lesser beats. And its great pain,
like its great joy, is too great for us.
So we always tear ourselves away again
and are only mouth.
    But suddenly the great
Heartbeat enters into us invisibly
and we cry out . . .
and then are being, change and countenance.
[Rilke¹]

'Being, change, and countenance', these are the three realities of dialogue which 'the great Heartbeat' of God introduced into the Roman Catholic Church through the prophetic inspiration of a pope and the eventual elaboration of a Council. Being is what we share both as creatures through our birth and as Christians through our baptism. Change is what we achieve through humility, through repentance, through conversion, through dialogue. Countenance is what we become through the unity and reconciliation of the face of Christ revealed in our faces as the communion of saints through the working of the Holy Spirit.

Readers who have survived and are still reading will perhaps be aware that the meaning and purpose of this book is to persuade that, as Christians, we have no option other than dialogue. Such dialogue should be third-degree dialogue, nothing less. The attempts of the Jewish philosopher, Martin Buber, to articulate such a reality in terms of 'friendship' is a starting-point for the length and breadth, the height and depth of the reality which we are called to embody both in our own personal lives and in the physiognomy of our various Churches. For Roman Catholics, the visionary who proclaimed this fact was Pope John XXIII, and the process which enshrined it in irrevocable articulation was the Second Vatican Council. Although this formulation may have been ambiguous, it is still a touchstone which prevents us from going back to monologue. The deed that was done in Vatican II was the crossing of a Rubicon, or Red Sea, which the people of God can never again reverse or revoke. We are committed to the mystery of our incontrovertible communion. Shackled together like prisoners in a chain gang, there is no escape for any of us until all of us agree to move together. We are, as Christians, an ongoing dialogue.

What do we mean by dialogue? We have been using the word for over twenty-six centuries. Universal use of it dating back to Plato's famous Socratic dialogues, imitated by Christians such as Peter Abelard and down through the ages, has not meant that either the literary form or the underlying idea were influential in the history of Christian thought. Roman Catholics were forbidden to take part in dialogue with other Christians until they were encouraged by Vatican II to engage with people of different denominations, other religions, or none at all. 'Such dialogue, *Gaudium et Spes* [#92] assured us, . . . excludes no one'. Is this something new?

Just as St John appropriated the Greek word '*logos*' and used it to describe a miraculous reality never before envisaged or contemplated in the history of the universe, so too Pope John XXIII inserted into the vocabulary of the Roman Catholic Church the word 'dialogue', which takes on a refurbished and mysterious meaning in its new surroundings and context. 'Suddenly the great Heartbeat enters into us invisibly and we cry out . . . and then are being, change and countenance.'

For these forty years after Vatican II the Roman Catholic Church has moved from an idiom of anathema to an idiom of dialogue. Instead of shunning and condemning heretics, pagans, schismatics, Catholics have been taught to engage in dialogue and refer instead to 'separated' brothers and sisters. Despite the ambiguity about the exact meaning of this term 'dialogue', it did succeed in introducing a hopeful atmosphere of irenicism in relations between the Roman Catholic Church and other Christian denominations. However, if dialogue is to relate in any way to the philosophical insights which incubated it as a twentieth-century revolution, then it must be understood not as an action, an attitude or an arrangement, which we as an organisation, might, or might not, make, it must be understood rather as the very being of what we are.

Essentially our being is mystery. It comes from the Father of all that is who is unknown, unknowable and never to be fully understood. Before this silent and unutterable mystery every human being is by definition agnostic. As Christians we have been given a glimpse of the Trinitarian God through the incarnation of the Son. Jesus Christ is the human face of the Trinity. He is therefore knowable as one of us. The danger is that we take this gift and turn it into a magic formula. We then become gnostics, those who claim to know; those with the secret knowledge of God unavailable to others outside our group. Whereas our Christianity should mean that we are neither gnostics nor agnostics, but rather diagnostics who can prescribe the way forward between the known and the unknown through the ongoing dialogue with each other in the Holy Spirit. The Holy Spirit as the third Person of the Trinity is the enzymatic aeration of our personhood which allows each of us to escape from the prison of individuality to enter the space of universality. This space beyond ourselves as limited insular provincials is the space of dialogue. 'Catholicism' originally meant respect for the whole of reality, all-inclusiveness [*Kata* = in respect of; *holos* = whole].

Dialogue is not an addition to what we already are, it is the transformation of what we are by nature to what we can become by Divine intervention. Christianity innoculates us against sectarianism by the open heart surgery which unhinges forever the otherwise asphyxiating rib-cage of tribal religion, denominational bigotry. Unless we accede to this openness, this dialogue, we cannot claim to be Christian. The Christian is by definition porous to the point of infinity. Bigotry, sectarianism, as natural religious manifestations are anti-Christian.

We are born sectarian. Biologically we are bigoted. It is now half a century since the discovery of DNA: deoxyribonucleic acid. This describes the chemical basis of the gene, found in the cell nucleus. As living things we are self-reproducing, self-maintaining mechanisms whose growth, development and reproduction are based on chemical information conveyed between generations of cells and organisms. This transmission from generation to generation ensures that we are tribal and sectarian by nature and from birth.

Other biological species, our natural companions on the planet, are entirely governed by these natural laws. We can escape them. We are the only creatures who are not completely governed by our DNA. Religion at its best, and Christianity as it should be, releases us from the prison of our nature, frees us from the narrowness of biology, introduces us to the freedom and fresh air of universality and infinity. We are invited to the dimensions of divinity. Through dialogue and the dialogical principle we can open ourselves up to the fullness of our potential being. Any dimension less than that is missing the mark, is the sin against the Spirit.

Culture is a thing we weave ourselves. The labyrinth as an image represents the complex structure of socio-political, religious, educational and psychological ideologies which we enter at birth as our cultural heritage and from which there is no easy escape. Culture is universal. Everyone of us comes wrapped inside it. It is also particular and local. It is different for every part of the planet and at every time a child is born. So, there can be no definitive antidote. Each manifestation of it requires the particular genius of the particular place to provide its own pioneering trail-blazers who can lead the people out of bondage. Each tribe has to give birth to its own Theseus to find its way out of the labyrinth which, of necessity, constitutes its cultural life-jacket.

'It is sufficient for one person to think', Edmund Husserl is reported to have said, 'for a whole generation to be saved.' But 'thinking' in this context has to be more than the logical workings of the culturally situated mind. It has to be the work of imagination. The work of a certain kind of person capable of imagining a brave new world quite different from the one into which he or she was born.

We become different from our neighbours, our ancestors, our households because we have made ourselves different. This difference has been a combination of environment and the human organism in a co-operative mutation. Those who have been most effective and inspirational in both detecting the changes necessary and imagining the adaptations to be accomplished have been artists and geniuses of one kind or another.

We are 'unfinished' animals who complete ourselves through culture. There is a difference between the evolutionary process which unfolded the animal, vegetable and mineral world and the world which is now in place, since humanity established itself and became the dominant species on the planet. Animals are determined by nature. They do nothing more than instinctively fulfil the pattern inscribed in their genes and chromosomes. They are DNA docile. Our DNA only provides us with a Lego set to build our own completion. Ours is not a blueprint encoded in our genes, it is the basic score for an unfinished symphony. We complete or finish ourselves through culture. We are what Clifford Geertz has called 'cultural artifacts'. We become who we are 'under the guidance of cultural patterns, historically created systems of meaning in terms of which we give form, order, point and direction to our lives.' Denominational religion is always one such cultural artifact. We have to win back for it the purity and originality which Christianity embodies in the person of Jesus Christ. This purification is achieved by dialogue. We get to the original meaning, the founding Spirit, the paradigmatic Person by humble and truthful dialogue.

We want naturally to be automatons, we prefer to have our schedule organized, we don't want to be overwhelmed by possibility. The forces of nature want to grow a roof over our heads where none was intended. We are naturally inclined to build elaborate nests, immovable dams, honeycombed hives and subterranean anthills. Our automatic response to complexity and danger is to construct an indestructible labyrinth around our deepest, most vulnerable and fragile self. We are all aware of this force of gravity in ourselves, the compelling drive towards universal compendiums and ungainsayable creeds. We long for the harmonious luxury of certitude expressed in 'the geometrical absolutism of an orthodoxy.'

Christianity is not a biological religion, it is an injection of divine life. It works against, transforms and overcomes every aspect and energy of 'natural' religion without thereby destroying the cultural artifacts and retrievable elements of any such transcendent aspiration. Christianity at its source and in its constitution is not a substance, a set of propositions, a formula of any kind. It is not a piece of property or a certified cure; not a guaranteed formula or indemnified insurance; not something which can be owned, controlled or guaranteed by anyone or any group. It is a possibility which is offered to anyone who is ready for it. The possibility is that of life. Life is something you either have or you have not. There is no in between. Either you are alive or you are not alive. If you have this life in you then you are a Christian. If you do have this life, then by its fruits you will be known. Love is the ultimate fruit of such life. Dialogue is a kind of loving, another fruit of divine life. Because Christianity is essentially relationship: relationship with God; relationship through Christ, with Christ and in Christ by the power of the Holy Spirit. The Church is a relationship between persons. It is founded on a person, by a person, through other particular persons. What the Church is, its reality, is handed on, handed down, from persons to persons in a relationship of faith, hope and love. The word to 'hand on' or 'hand down' from which our word 'tradition' derives is the same word in Latin for 'betrayal'. Jesus was handed over by Judas to persons who would murder him. We either hand on life or we hand on its opposite, which is death. Such a tradition would be equivalent to murder. We were given life and we destroyed it. Christianity without dialogue is Christianity annihilated.

Our dialogue between Christians is not about a written text, it is about a living reality. In our dialogue as Christians we have no mandate to focus all our critical faculties on words or formulae which come down to us as more or less adequate encapsulations of the truth which is incarnate in the person of Jesus Christ. All such written texts are secondary theology in comparison with the primary theology which is unwritten and requires spiritual transmission from person to person because it is an essentially inexpressible mystery. All our formulae are paradigms of a deeper reality which Christians who have preceded us have tried to express by the enlightening power of the Holy Spirit. Our dialogue, which necessarily involves our study of such dogmatic formulae, cannot focus exclusively on such texts, it must concentrate also upon the reality, the Person, the relationship which seeks expression therein. The word 'dogma' in Greek means 'that which seems right' and has come to mean a proposition which is to be believed by Catholics as having been divinely revealed and which cannot be denied without falling into heresy. So be it. The word 'heresy' comes from the Greek word meaning 'to select', to section yourself off from the fullness of truth. No Christian wants to do this. That is why it is imperative for all Christians to enter into dialogue about the full meaning of the mystery which we all believe in, and which it is our privilege to find enunciated in many and various ways throughout the two-thousand-year history of this Tradition. There can be only one, holy, catholic and apostolic Church of Christ which we would all wish to belong to as it holds the tradition within its unity: meaning the knowledge in the Holy Spirit of the Incarnate Word. As disciples of Christ in dialogue we cannot afford to situate ourselves exclusively in front of any text, any written words, we have to situate ourselves together in the space between those formulae and the living persons who are the authors, the objects and the only purpose of any such credal expressions.

The phenomenological movement in philosophy in the twentieth century opened to us the possibility of understanding ourselves as human beings, no longer in terms of individual substances, as in Aristotelian metaphysics, but in terms of relationship. Relationship is the ultimate category of human being. This underpins the 'personalist' movement in philosophy which in turn gave birth to the twentieth-century notion of dialogue, which was revolutionary in its constitution and its scope. Dialogue became ripe for plucking as further expression of the Christian mystery and Pope John XXIII was open to the prompting of the Holy Spirit to appropriate this very potent sign of the times.

'In the beginning was the word (*logos*)' we are told in the first words of the 'prologue' of St John's Gospel. All things were made by that word or logos and through (*dia*) that word (*logos*) was made all things that were made. We are, therefore, a *dia-logue* from the beginning of time. No one is excluded. All things that are, came to be, received their being, through (*dia*) that word (*logos*). Could anything be clearer? Dialogue is what we are because that is the way we were made.

Even our own words are realities which define us. Earthly speech is not simply given to us with our physical birth. We undergo a second birth. This, if you like, can be called the birth of the soul. But whatever we care to call it, it means that we gain the ability to speak under the influence of a human ambience. 'Without human beings around us we would not stand upright. Without this upright posture, our hands would have had to carry our body; they would not be free for the *expression* of the soul, which is born in uttering itself. Pointing, indicating, grasping and wanting to grasp are the first appearance of speech and are, at the same time, the whole of speech. *Whoever* is able to point to something, speaks, and has all that is necessary for speaking: *I, You, That*: Cognition'.[2] Our entry into this world forces us to become creatures of dialogue. We share what we have inherited with one another by pointing towards what we perceive and agreeing upon sounds and vocables which best describe these realities.

Two things become apparent from this juxtaposition: it is the world itself that makes us speak, that provides us with the wherewithal of our dialogue.

> The world speaks: this, that. Man hears it and is capable of perceiving the speaking itself, which (or who) makes this and that into *this* and *that*. The Logos is invisible, imperceptible to the senses. It is the invisible one; it is as invisible as the speaker in man: you do not see him either. For the speaker in us is not mouth, tongue, face, head, hand etc. These are the means of expression, we move them. All speaking is movement: movement for the sake

of expression. Even no movement – silence – can become speech.[3]

We speak the world by giving names to the 'this' and 'that' we see and hear, taste, touch and smell what is around us. But our language is secondary, it is our blundering way of putting words on the primary 'logos' revealed in the world we share. Which brings us to the second truth: 'Whoever can speak is not of this world. *This* world exists *for* and *through* the speaker, through the Logos. Nothing is un-sayable; it is a Logos-world.'[4] We, as speakers, are both outside and inside this world. We are strangers in one sense *because* we can speak. Language, the logos, differentiates us from every other reality in the world. Only humans can speak, because only humans have privileged access to the Logos: 'No one can learn a language who cannot already speak, who does not already have the undifferentiated predisposition for any language. This is the primal speech of which each individual language is a particular crystallized form.'[5]

We are children of the Logos. History has taught us with heart-rending examples that the language instinct in each one of us is primary. In the infamous Atlantic slave trade on the tobacco, cotton, coffee and sugar plantations, greedy landowners would put to work slaves of different ethnicities to get more work and less talk out of them. 'When speakers of different languages have to communicate to carry out practical tasks ... they develop a make-shift jargon called a pidgin.'[6] These are sometimes haphazard strings of words borrowed from the language of the colonizers or plantation owners. In certain places this 'Pidgin' can become a *lingua franca*.

The third reality, which devolves from this phenomenon of language, is that whoever speaks must be someone. In Buber's terminology whoever speaks in this way is a person. Dialogue makes us persons. As persons we are already in such dialogue. This is what Christianity came to make fully real. This dialogue is, in a certain sense, Christianity. It is the dialogue which continues forever between the three persons of the Trinity and which Jesus Christ came on earth to translate into a human idiom. We, as Churches have elaborated our own Pidgin Theology.

Our dialogue is in and through the Holy Spirit. And as Karl Rahner puts it: 'In the Spirit of God all of us "know" something more simple, more true and more real than we can know or express at the level of our theological concepts.'[7] Dialogue is showing, pointing towards, sharing the things which we surmise, rather than the creeds which we have formulated. Our dialogue should be about the reality which we have inherited rather than about the 'pidgin' which we have invented to express this.

> If I want to make myself understood by a Japanese and we know no common language, I will point to the sky, saying 'sky,' and ask him with a gesture what 'that' is called in his language. He understands me and says his word. *What* did he understand? *What* do we have in common? I point to *that*, the sky, and he understands that this *that* is the sky – not the air, not the blue, etc. We understood each other without words: he grasped which *that* I was pointing to and this that was already word, beyond any particular language. He grasped the *real* word, pure understanding, of which every sign, every spoken word, is only an indication. Such wordless understanding makes translation possible. It makes a thing a *thing*. This wordless word is not an outer "name" attached to a thing, it *is* the thing.[8]

How true this is of all that we 'know' about Christianity, about the incarnation, about the resurrection, about the Trinity, about the Eucharist. Such dialogue unites us as Christians and as human beings and involves us in a kind of dialogue with other world religions also where a similar kind of communication is also present:

> We find similar structures in Zen Buddhist stories. Here the student's questions are met by the master's apparently irrelevant answers and sometimes even with blows – either of which is intended to draw attention away from the content of the discourse and to focus instead on the speaking, the dialogue as such, the happening between I and you. In a wider sense even a blow is a sign, meaning: I have heard you, and you hear me. Sometimes, the dialogue is suddenly interrupted by the question: What is that? Even though Zen Buddhism is active today, it is nevertheless pre-Christian in its attitude towards consciousness. Its central intention is to point to the word, not by teaching in words, but by realising the presence of the word between human beings, and by directing the attention to the still living, floating word.[9]

Karl Rahner suggests that our dialogue, as Christians, should concentrate on the future rather than on the past. If we try to develop together a theology of Christianity which will speak to the people of today and tomorrow this should help us to move closer together in the formulation of what we hold in common and what we understand as the mystery which unites us.[10] Doing ecumenical theology in this indirect way, more appropriate to a 'post-Christian' era, will make us aware of our differences in ways that will help us also to overcome these.

The Church of Christ is founded on a silent personal mystery which can never be translated adequately into human words. All speech about this reality is necessarily fumbling: a stab at the truth. Tradition of the mystery always risks betrayal. And yet we have to formulate the *mirabilia dei* into some enduring shape so that it is never forgotten and so that it can be passed on from generation to generation. However, like the written notation which preserves great musical works, the encodement is nothing without the music which must be realised in every generation. Unless the music is actually heard it remains a disembodied skeleton in the score. Similarly, all credal formulae, dogmatic tracts, articles of faith, articulations of the mysteries of Christianity, are humble servants of a much greater and quite other reality which no person in the world can claim as a possession. No person or people, no Church or catechism, no dogma or denomination incorporates the mystery of our faith. Definitive incorporation of this mystery took place in the person of Jesus Christ. Post-Christian elaboration of this visitation must be the work of the Holy Spirit.

The word 'person' in the Christian context is unrecognisable from its normal usage in any other context. The person, whether divine or human, is unrepeatable, unique, original, sui generis, matchless, peerless, exceptional and eternal. To achieve personhood we have to escape from the biological individuality which makes us children of the natural world. Our DNA allows us to survive as biological creatures whose natural law is described by T. S. Eliot as 'birth, copulation, and death'. The instinct of preservation, the endurance of the species, the survival of the fittest, such natural reflexes have allowed us to evolve and to dominate as one among many predators on the planet. What allowed us to survive must be transmogrified if we are to recover from survival. To escape from this natural horizontal time and space bound dimension we need divine intervention. This is the reality of Christianity. Being, as defined by biology is raised [resurrection] to the level of 'forever-well-being' in the Holy Spirit. This metamorphosis of our nature from caterpillar to butterfly, from finite to infinite, from horizontal to vertical, from natural to divine is the full realization of personhood. The person is free from ties to nature, from restriction of time and space, from limitation of local or tribal circumvention: person means accession to the divine, to dialogue with the three persons of the everlasting Trinity. That is why the person is called to relationship with God because at this level both are equal. Persons as infinite, as everlasting, as unique are all equal to one another. The Father as person, the Son as person, and the Holy Spirit as person, not only relate to one another as persons in dialogue, but each of them also relates to each one of us also as persons. We are called to participate in this relationship as equals. Every person is equal, because unique, at the level of love. Dialogue with God, as prayer, is participating in the life of the Trinity, communicating in this idiom.

And conversation is similar to the Latin word *conversatio,* which means the turning around of true repentance. This is the second movement of the trio: Being, *change* and countenance. Such turning is reaching this profoundest level of our own being as person. Our connection with each other is not the joining of hands around the periphery of a circle, horizontally orchestrated happy-clappy well-being among ourselves, it is the communion we achieve as points connected through the radius to the centre of the circle around which we stand in conversation with, through, and in the Holy Spirit.

We already are the reality which we share together in dialogue. We are not trying to move from complete division to unity, but from one kind of unity to another. We are trying to move from inarticulate unity to agreed unity. Our words are third-hand attempts to sketch the unimaginable. The original word [logos] of our dialogue was made flesh in the incarnate word, Christ Jesus, and he again made his flesh word in the Gospels. We make his words flesh in our persons as baptised and believing Christians, named after his name, his word made flesh and again made word in this nominative vocable. And we again turn this enfleshed faith into stumbling words when we dialogue with each other about the mystery which makes us what we are. We share a common heritage as Christians: the

Scriptures, the Apostle's Creed, the Councils of Nicea and Constantinople already form a substantial platform of potential unity. But we may have to start the work of faithful tradition all over again until we all understand and agree to what has been formulated.

The Holy Spirit is the Person of the Trinity who achieves or accomplishes this translation into words by the Spirit's personal infusion to the point of interpenetration of each one of our persons. Whereas Christ, the second Person of the Trinity, became incarnate in our human nature, the Holy Spirit, as Third Person of the Trinity, impregnates our person. This is the mystery of Pentecost, the most inexplicable reality about who we really are. So, dialogue for the Christian is the listening and the speaking of the Holy Spirit to the Holy Spirit in each of the persons so engaged. The process of dialogue is therefore learning the humility which allows the Holy Spirit to speak through my spirit when I am engaged with another person in such ecumenical dialogue. The result of such reciprocated inspiration can never be predetermined; part of the humility involved must be the readiness to hear something which takes us beyond anything we had previously contemplated or imagined. Individuals, whether as separate people or as separated Churches, are condemned to monologue; persons are open to dialogue.

We do not have something which makes us a Church; there is no substance which can be identified as the reality we have to protect or safeguard as we move into communion with each other. Our being as Church is relationship; dialogue is the most fundamental reality of who and what we are. Christ is the way, the truth and the life. We dialogue in order to accomplish these realities. They are verified, validated, by our incarnation of them. Life is apparent in the persons of those who are living it, those who are alive. Truth is something we acknowledge as growth within ourselves. It is the tree of life growing as our communion together before our eyes. To live something else, something different, is to cut ourselves off from the vine which is our source of life. Any so-called Church which is established independently of this source is not alive, is not Christian, has no access to divine life. Any group of people gathered in his name are guaranteed to be 'Churches' because he is present, his spirit is present. Anything less than this is heresy, falsehood. We can be a club, a cabal, a congregation. If we want to belong to the one Church of Christ we have to be permeated by His divine life made present in and through the Holy Spirit. Such realities are visible in their fruits. By these fruits shall we know them. Stunted growth, failure to live, means that we have lost our way.

All of this should point towards a much greater trust in and reliance upon the Holy Spirit as both the source and the goal of our ecumenical dialogue. This Holy Spirit would be seen not only as the instigator of a new movement within the Churches, but also as the goal of all such dialogue. For, after all, the Church's one foundation is Jesus Christ, Our Lord, and the true face of Christ is revealed to us only through the Holy Spirit. This same Holy Spirit is said to have no face apart from the final revelation of that face in and through the united faces of all those members of Christ's mystical body, which will be revealed in the final realization of God's eschatological embodiment. The mirror of that face, within the earthly Church of Christ, has been irreparably damaged by the disunity of that Church, and can only be repaired and reconstituted as an effective mirror through the restoration or reinvention of visible unity.

The steps which the Catholic Church has taken in the past half century to accept some of the blame for the present state of disunity, to recognize the dignity and the good will of those who presently find themselves in Christian communities no longer united with Rome, and to accept that the Holy Spirit is alive and active in the life and liturgy of these Churches, are certainly an advance on the road to Christian unity, which must be the goal of every committed Christian. However, the question is whether or not the Roman Catholic Church is being asked by that same Holy Spirit, and has already been induced to admit through the voice of the Second Vatican Council, which records the divine impulse of that time, to undertake an even more profound conversion and enter more deeply and perhaps less cautiously into the purifying stream of dialogue.

Judeo-Christianity is a specific religion different from other religions on this earth because it stems not from our nature or our earth, but from a call to exodus from that nature to another kind of existence, which is divine. This does not mean that it is any less careful or appreciative of the earth, the world, the nature which produced it; it means another kind of relationship, a relationship of dialogue with our nature, our world, our mother earth. This in turn means that it cannot view all other religions in the world as equal or as equivalent to itself. Nothing less than the full revelation of the one true God and the establishment of relationship with that God in right worship – the meaning of 'orthodoxy' – is 'religion' in the full reality of that word. Other religions can be close to, distant from, this reality, but without the power of God's love circulating in our veins we are deprived, we are outside, the true religion, the meaning of life, the highest form of life itself. The life and love of everlasting divinity is unmistakeable, irreplaceable, identifiable. There is no substitute.

Judeo-Christianity in this sense is always exigently critical. It can appropriate, accommodate anything it finds in any other religion but unless it recognises the full length and breadth, height and depth of the Love of God revealed in Jesus Christ and made present by, with and through the Holy Spirit, it cannot confirm any other religion as authentic and life-giving. So, there is a difference between dialogue between Judeo-Christians among themselves and dialogue between Judeo-Christianity and other world religions.

The branch of Judeo-Christianity which is the Roman Catholic Church may once have claimed that it alone was the true channel of the Holy Spirit, that outside its fold there was no salvation. Since Vatican Council II it can no longer do so. It has been established dogmatically that the Holy Spirit can and does blow where that Spirit wills. Christianity exists in places other than and outside the Roman Catholic Church.

The phrase 'subsists in', which the Vatican Council used to express the double truth that the Spirit of Christianity resides in a guaranteed fashion within the Roman Catholic Church while, at the same time, not being exclusively owned by that denomination, is essentially a 'scholastic' term, coming from Medieval theology.[11] Its purpose in this context was not to define the way in which the full truth of Judeo-Christianity is distributed throughout the world, and within other Christian denominations in particular, rather was it to guarantee to Roman Catholics that whatever else it might say, this formula was assuring them that adherence to the Roman Catholic Church itself could provide them with assured and uncontaminated access to the way, the truth and the life of the three persons of the triune God. Subsistence implies a form that is imbued with being. This does not suggest that it is the only form so endowed, it merely affirms that the full truth of Judeo-Christianity can be accessed through this particular manifestation, no matter how unlikely or distorted this may seem to be from the outside. Catholics are guaranteed the real presence of the triune God in the tradition which they have inherited. This guarantee is in no way exclusive, nor does it justify or endorse every manifestation, historical accretion or idiosyncratic devotion of Roman Catholicism. It offers a possibility, the possibility of life and love in its fullest manifestation. It says that you can find, if you look closely enough, the whole truth of the Divine Self-Revelation, in the fundamental infrastructure of this particular tradition. To turn this guarantee into an absolutistic monopoly is to overreach its mandate and risk betrayal of the most precious of its energies: which are the *viscera misericordiae Dei*.

In the light of all that has been said in Chapter Three of this book, it may be too simplistic to say that dialogue is incumbent upon every Judeo-Christian, that such dialogue with non-Judeo-Christians may be 'abstract', but that dialogue between Judeo-Christians must be 'concrete'. But it is a start. It is a sketch-map, which can then be refined or discarded as the dialogue advances. The question as to whether the 'concrete' dialogue between fellow Judeo-Christians is 'educational' dialogue or the dialogue of 'friendship' is another possible framework for clarifying our ecumenism.

My own view is that Jesus Christ himself has told us that such dialogue is, by definition, a dialogue of friendship: 'I call you friends because I have made known to you everything that I have heard from my Father'(Jn. 15:15). The reason for this friendship is that 'my Father will love them, and we will come to them and make our home with them' (Jn. 14:23). Our dialogue can be nothing less than the dialogue continually subsisting in the Godhead between the three persons of the Trinity. We become 'persons' only as fully participating members of that dialogue which constitutes the one true Church of Judeo-Christianity. Our dialogue of 'friendship' is one that helps us to accomplish that end fully, to cast aside anything which might impede us or stand in our way, to understand whatever it is that we must understand in order to allow us to achieve such full communion.

In such dialogue of friendship even the most thorny matters of contention can be approached in humility and the desire for truth. I end this chapter with an example of such dialogue which I experienced twenty years ago.[12] Here Bishop Kallistos Ware[13] is talking with Professor Dermot Moran[14] and myself about the Petrine Ministry, the possibility of the whole of Christianity being united under one Pope:

> *Bishop Kallistos Ware:* For the Orthodox in a reunited Christendom there is no doubt at all that the Bishop of

Rome, the Pope would have the first place. That was the pattern in the ancient Christian world. This is the pattern to which we would return but we, on the Orthodox side, tend to think of the primacy of the Pope, if you like, as a primacy of honour. I would rather say a primacy of service. We are not so keen these days about honour, so a primacy of service, a primacy of love. Saint Ignatius of Antioch addresses the Church of Rome as the Church which presides in love and that is a phrase that the Orthodox often like to quote. What troubles us is that it seems that this primacy of service, primacy of love, has been turned into a primacy of power and of jurisdiction. We are ready to give, in a reunited Christendom, an all-embracing pastoral care to the Pope, but we would still believe that the Church on Earth is essentially a conciliar Church. Therefore, when problems arise, they are normally solved through the meeting of a council, through a synod, which is a continuation of the mystery of Pentecost. We meet together, pray to the Holy Spirit and seek to reach a common mind. In the synod, the Pope would have the first place, but he would be a member with his brother bishops. So we see the Pope essentially as the first among equals.

Professor Dermot Moran: Well, taking up your phrase of a reunited Christendom, it occurs to me that although there may be reconciliation between the Roman Catholic and the Orthodox Churches, perhaps under the recognition of the Pope in some sort of headship, wouldn't that create great problems then with many of the Protestant Churches in their own relationship with whatever the new Catholic-Orthodox Church would wish to call itself: The One Holy Catholic and Apostolic Church presumably?

K W: I wonder. I don't think it would create difficulties with the Anglicans. They would be willing to take the same kind of view as the Orthodox, to have the Pope as the elder brother within the Christian world. And perhaps many of the Protestant Churches, now we are putting aside the polemics of the past, also see the need for a certain visible primacy of the Church on Earth, and see that this need not conflict with the fact that we all recognise Jesus Christ as the head of the Church.

If the primacy of Peter, the primacy of the Pope, is presented in strictly juridical terms then I think we shall have difficulties, but if it is presented in pastoral terms as it is now being presented more and more by Catholic spokesmen, then there is a real possibility of meeting together because very widely in the Christian world today people can see the need for a certain primacy of pastoral initiative. If it is not spelt out in legalistic terms, but in terms of mutual love, if your model is Christ washing the feet of his disciples, Christ saying, 'the Kings of the Gentiles give orders to their servants but it shall not be so among you'. If that is our model, then there need not be a problem.

D M: What are the advantages to be gained by a merger or a union, a reunion of the Churches, Bishop Kallistos?

K W: On the Orthodox side, particularly in recent centuries, we have suffered in our Church life from excessive nationalism. In theory, we have spoken of ourselves as the Catholic Church, but in practice, the vision of very many Orthodox has been limited simply to their own nation. They have thought of themselves being Greek Orthodox with the emphasis on Greek, Russian or Serbian Orthodox with the emphasis on themselves as particular nationalities rather than as members of the Universal Orthodox Catholic Church. The different national Churches have been, to a large extent, isolated from one another. In the modern world, this is not sufficient. We belong to a shrinking world, we all need each other and national isolation is not really a possibility. So we feel the need for a greater visible unity and a more direct expression of that unity and that has made many of us feel that we do need the element of primacy. This is partly provided by the Patriarch of Constantinople at the moment, but it could be provided much more fully and universally if we could have unity with the Catholic Church in the west and if the symbol of primacy were to be at Rome.

Christian unity does not mean the imposition of a single pattern. Certainly, it does not mean a centralised administration. We want to unite in all the distinctive riches of our own traditions and perhaps one of the best effects of ecumenism could be that by learning about other Churches, we could look with new eyes at our own traditions and for the first time see what is really there. The value of a journey is that you come back to your home and see it with fresh eyes and that could be what ecumenism does for us.

Notes

1   This poem by Rainer Maria Rilke was written in Schönech, September 1923 'for Frau Agnes Renold'. The translation is by Christopher Bamford.
2   *Becoming Aware of the Logos, The Way of St John the Evangelist*, by Georg Kühlewind. Edited and translated by Christopher Bamford, p. 17.
3   Ibid., p. 21.
4   Kühlewind op. cit., p. 19.
5   Ibid., p. 18.
6   Steven Pinker, *The Language Instinct*, Penguin Books, 1994, p. 32ff.
7   Karl Rahner, *Theological Investigations* 14, p. 251.
8   Kühlewind, op. cit., p. 16.
9   Ibid., p. 59.

10   Karl Rahner, *TI*, pp. 252-3.

11   The idea originally conveyed by the Latin word *'subsistere'* was 'to halt'. But as a technical term in scholastic theology it was used, according to Boethius [*Liber de Persona et Duabus Naturis*, c.III; PL, LXIV, 1344B], to translate the Greek *'ousiôsthai'* 'to be endowed with being'. Cf Joseph Owens, *An Elementary Christian Metaphysics*, The Bruce Publishing Company, Milwaukee, 1963, pp. 151-154.

12   This dialogue was organised by Dermot Moran, now Professor of Philosophy, Chair of Metaphysics and Logic at University College Dublin. It took place between Bishop Kallistos Ware and the author of this book. It was intended as part of a series to be broadcast on Radio Éireann in 1984. This excerpt from the tape recording of our talks is reproduced with kind permission of both participants and of Malachy Moran, of RTÉ Sound Archive.

13   Bishop Kallistos Ware was born Timothy Ware, in Bath, Somerset, in 1934 and was educated at Westminster School and Magdalen College, Oxford, where he took a Double First in Classics, as well as reading Theology. After joining the Orthodox Church in 1958, he travelled widely in Greece, staying in particular at the monastery of St John, Patmos, and he is familiar with the life of other Orthodox centres such as Mount Athos and Jerusalem. In 1966 he was ordained priest and became a monk, receiving the new name 'Kallistos'. Since 1966 he has been back at Oxford as Spalding Lecturer in Eastern Orthodox Studies at the University. He also has pastoral charge of the Greek parish in Oxford. In 1970 he became a Fellow of Pembroke College, Oxford. In 1982 he was consecrated titular Bishop of Diokleia and appointed Assistant Bishop in the Orthodox Archdiocese of Thyateira and Great Britain (under the Ecumenical Patriarchate).

14   Dermot Moran is Professor of Philosophy, Chair of Metaphysics and Logic at University College Dublin, Ireland, where he is the editor of the *International Journal of Philosophical Studies*.